Wendy Richardson continues to blaze new trails in the uncharted territory of AD/HD and addictive behavior. She opens new avenues of hope and help with her latest book. Outstanding!

—MICHELLE NOVOTNI, PH.D., psychologist, international lecturer, author of *Adult AD/HD* and *What Does Everybody Else Know that I Don't?*

This book is a wonderful guide for professionals to use with clients and to help adults come to terms with their own challenges.

—SARI SOLDEN, MS

As an Addiction Professional and the parent of an AD/HD daughter, Wendy Richardson has created concrete answers for a most frustrating mental disorder—"progress, not perfection."

—DELBERT B. BOONE, B.S. (Book-subject, Troubled Teens, Troubled Parents), Videos (Psychology of Addiction, Marijuana, Sobriety, Straight Up, Hip Hop Sobriety, Goin' Home To Stay) Multiple Telly Award winner

This very readable work provides one of the best guides for all those who help on the path to recovery from AD/HD.

—Dwaine McCallon, MD, former assistant chief medical officer of the Colorado Department of Corrections, author of *Treatable Criminal Minds*

Wendy Richardson's new book, *When Too Much Isn't Enough*, is a must-read for anyone impacted by ADD and/or addictions.

—Kate Kelly & Peggy Ramundo, authors of *You Mean I'm Not Lazy, Stupid Or Crazy?!* and *The ADDed Dimension*, Founders of ADDed Dimension Coaching Group, www.addcoaching.com

ENDING THE DESTRUCTIVE CYCLE
OF AD/HD AND ADDICTIVE BEHAVIOR

WHEN
TOO
MUCH
ISN'T ENOUGH

WENDY RICHARDSON, MA

OUR GUARANTEE TO YOU

We believe so strongly in the message of our books that we are making this quality guarantee to you. If for any reason you are disappointed with the content of this book, return the title page to us with your name and address and we will refund to you the list price of the book. To help us serve you better, please briefly describe why you were disappointed. Mail your refund request to: Piñon Press, P.O. Box 35002, Colorado Springs, CO 80935.

ISBN 1-57683-631-2

Cover design by Arvid Wallen
Creative Team: Nicci Jordan, Rachelle Gardner, Darla Hightower, Arvid Wallen,
    Pat Miller, Tyler Willis Richardson
Interior illustrations by Cynthia S. Brown

Some of the anecdotal illustrations in this book are true to life and are included with the permission of the persons involved. All other illustrations are composites of real situations, and any resemblance to people living or dead is coincidental.

Richardson, Wendy, 1954-
  When too much isn't enough : ending the destructive cycle of AD/HD and addictive behavior / by Wendy Richardson.
    p. cm.
  Includes bibliographical references and index.
  ISBN 1-57683-631-2
  1. Attention-deficit disorder in adults. 2. Compulsive behavior. 3. Substance abuse.
I. Title.

  RC394.A85R533 2005
  616.85'89--dc22

                          2004021284

Printed in Canada

1 2 3 4 5 6 7 8 9 10 / 08 07 06 05 04 05

When Too Much Isn't Enough
is dedicated to my mother
JoAnne J. Willis,
who lived with my father's
untreated AD/HD and addiction
and single-handedly
parented three children,
two of whom have AD/HD.
Thank you, Mom,
for giving me your best.

CONTENTS

ACKNOWLEDGMENTS

AS AN AUTHOR WITH AD/HD and learning disabilities, it took support and help from family, friends, and colleagues to make this book possible. I want to express my deepest appreciation to each and every one of you for your contributions. Thank you to my editor, Rachelle Gardner, for her ongoing support, sense of humor, and guidance as I rewrote this manuscript again and again. I appreciate all the people at Piñon Press for their kindness and enthusiasm about this book.

Thank you, Eric, for your support and additional parenting of our children, as well as the many hours you spent diligently proofreading the manuscript. Special thanks to my daughter Lindsey for her inspiration, support, and understanding. To my son Tyler for his research skills and contribution to the cover design of this book. Thank you both for your patience when my writing took me away from you. I am blessed to be your mother.

Special appreciation goes to my colleague Richard Gilbert, M.D., for his help with the medication chapter of this book, as well as Martin Teicher, Ph.D., M.D., for his research and ability to help me write about technical aspects of neuroscience in ways that are understandable. I especially want to thank Dwaine McCallon, M.D., for his valuable contributions to the chapters on medications and co-occurring conditions, and for being the big brother I've always wanted. Thank you, Cynthia S. Brown, artist and rock-climbing partner, for drawing the illustrations in this book. Special appreciation goes to Ms. Sydney Sauber, M.Ed., Ed.S., for the many hours of listening, brainstorming, and feedback you so freely gave.

I also want to thank the following people for their personal and professional contributions: Zachary Alaxander, Carol C. Anderson, Esq., Anthony Boken, Molly Burke, Lori Butterworth, David E. Comings, M.D., Jim Daniels, Thom Franklin, MBA,

Gail Griffith, Frank Giuliani, Pharm.D., Kate Kelly, RN, MSN, D. Steven Ledingham, Jenell Murphy, M.Ed., LPC, Michelle Novotni, Ph.D., Nancy Ratey, Ed.M., John J. Ratey, M.D., Susan Tatsui-D'Arcy, Janet Rupp, and the Aptos Serenity Group.

I thank the many people with AD/HD and co-occurring conditions who shared their experiences, frustrations, shame, tenacity, creativity, and journey of recovery with me. You are my teachers. This book would not be what it is without you!

1

how
this
book
will
help
you

CUT TO
THE CHASE

HAVE YOU SPENT GOOD portions of your life unsuccessfully try-ing to control your eating, drinking, or drug use? Do you struggle to manage overspending, gambling, excessive Internet use, or your sexual behavior?

Is it hard for you to focus your attention? Are you easily bored? Do you have problems organizing your life? Do you have a body or brain that's always on the go, or on the other hand, is it difficult for you to get going and keep going? If these questions strike a chord with you, untreated Attention-Deficit/Hyperactivity Disorder (AD/HD) may be contributing to your overindulging or addiction.

The purpose of this book is to help you understand how and why people with AD/HD overindulge and become addicted, and how to get out of the vicious cycle of self-medicating your symp-toms with drugs, food, alcohol, and compulsive behaviors. We'll look at the ways AD/HD intersects and overlaps with substance misuse, and you'll learn about similarities and shared character-istics of AD/HD and addiction. For example, you will understand how a woman with AD/HD, clean and sober for years and with no alcohol or drugs in her system, flunks a field sobriety test.

Let's start with a brief overview of how some AD/HD symp-toms are similar to those of overindulging and addiction, as well as how they can contribute to each other.

SELF-MEDICATING

We are self-medicating when we use substances and behaviors to help us feel better. There is a big difference between enjoying a glass of wine after a hectic day and needing a drink to cope with the day and be able to sleep. Our bodies and minds develop cravings. We become obsessed with thinking about when we can smoke pot or binge on junk food. We can't get enough. But there comes a point when self-medicating stops working. No matter how much we eat, purge, drink, or drug, we don't feel better. Instead, we feel worse. We can't eat another bite, drink another drink, or use another drug. Yet we do, because even too much isn't enough.

LOSS OF CONTROL

AD/HD, overindulging in substances, and compulsive behaviors all have one thing in common: loss of control. You can't manage your eating, drinking, drug use, or behavior. Loss of control over parts of your life, combined with the pain and frustration of AD/HD symptoms, can lead to self-medicating with substances and behaviors. If you have AD/HD, you may be living in a vicious cycle. Here's a brief overview of how AD/HD contributes to loss of control.

Attention
AD/HD makes it difficult to focus and keep your attention where you want it. You may be easily distracted, and/or your attention may be captured and you can't pull yourself away from the computer, TV, or project you are working on. It's also hard to be present and pay attention to the task at hand if you're obsessed with thoughts of bingeing, getting drunk, smoking pot, or having sex.

Impulse control
AD/HD hinders the control of impulses. It may be hard or impossible for you to control an impulse to overeat, binge on sweets, use alcohol or other drugs, spend money, gamble, or engage in high-risk behavior. Words may fly from your mouth before your mind has the chance to censor them. Taking drugs and drinking alcohol can decrease anyone's ability to control their impulses, but when drugs and alcohol are mixed with AD/HD, just about anything can happen.

Activity Level

You don't have to be hyperactive to have AD/HD. You may have an average activity level or you may even have a very low activity level. It may be difficult for you to get up in the morning and maintain enough energy to get through the day. You might have a hyperactive brain that constantly demands novel and stimulating input or never stops yakking at you. Your body could be restless and desire constant motion from your head to your toes. Because AD/HD contributes to problems with energy level, it is common for people to use substances to either stimulate or relax themselves. Ironically, people who are hyperactive are sometimes accused of being on cocaine or "speed," while some with low-energy AD/HD are accused of smoking pot or taking "downers," even though they're not.

Self-Activating and Organizing

Self-activating is the process of getting yourself going and moving in the direction you need to be moving in. It may be difficult for you to organize yourself so you can get to work or school and follow through with the demands of your day. You may be a great fifty-yard dasher but not be able to complete two miles, let alone a marathon. Life is filled with marathons, such as finishing school, maintaining your career and relationships, and parenting. If you have AD/HD or an alcohol, food, or drug problem, self-activating and organizing may be impossible, and you may live in chaos.

Cognitive Problems

Memory is frequently a problem for the AD/HD brain. You may remember specific details from years ago but not remember why you walked into a room or where you put your keys. It may be difficult for you to remember what you read or what you learned in a class or workshop. The same is true for those who misuse substances. They may have memory retrieval problems, blackouts, or in more serious cases, permanent brain damage.

Enhanced Sensitivity

You may be irritated by sights or sounds that others barely notice. The tags in your clothing or seams in your socks can drive you nuts. You live in a world that feels as though the lighting and sound have been turned up. You may have a heightened response to feedback from others, and you may take on the feelings of others without even knowing it. This enhanced sensitivity is common for some with AD/HD, and these characteristics are also reported by some people who misuse substances. As with other characteristics of AD/HD, you can have enhanced sensitivity without having AD/HD or abusing substances.

Sleep

As we learn more about AD/HD, many professionals are agreeing that sleep disturbances are a key component. You may be a "night owl" and have difficulty shutting your brain off so you can get to sleep, or you may wake frequently during the night and have difficulties falling back to sleep. For some with AD/HD, getting up in the morning is torture. Many who abuse substances also report chronic sleeping problems that can persist years into recovery or until treated.

THE BOTTOM LINE

If you think you have Attention-Deficit/Hyperactivity Disorder (AD/HD) and you also struggle to control your eating, drinking, or problematic behaviors, this book will help you.

HOW WILL THIS BOOK HELP?

This book was not written to make you feel worse than you already do. I wrote this book to help you find answers. What I offer is information, encouragement, and practical suggestions to help you cope effectively. Take what works for you. Allow yourself to start reading anywhere you like and skip parts if they're not helpful.

The stories people have volunteered to share with you are powerful and enlightening, but if you're not a story person, feel free to skip them. It's not important that you digest every word and concept in this book. I rarely read a book from cover to cover.

I wrote this book to help you accept who you are, including your AD/HD, overindulging, and addiction. It isn't until we accept that we have problems that we can get help for them. My number one suggestion is this: Give yourself permission to read at your own pace, in your own style. You may want to read the last chapter first. Underline, highlight, fold pages (unless you borrowed the book from a friend or the library), or use sticky notes to mark places.

This book is for those of you who are overindulging or addicted. It's also for those of you who have tried, and continue to try, to control your behavior and substance use, and for those of you who are in recovery. Oftentimes people need a period of recovery to realize that they have co-occurring conditions. AD/HD is one of many co-occurring conditions that may keep you from attaining your goals.

Perhaps you don't suffer from untreated AD/HD, overindulging, or addictions, but you work with or love someone who does. This book is for you too. With this information, you will be better able to understand and offer support and encouragement to your loved one, coworker, or friend.

This book is based on the research and opinions of many experts in the AD/HD, eating disorder, and addiction fields who provide new information almost on a daily basis. By the time you read this book there will be more exciting new information. This book is also based on my personal and professional experience, and the experiences of other people who have AD/HD and addictions. Together we provide you with knowledge, tools, experience, strength, and hope for a better life. While addictions and AD/HD may never be cured, you can learn to treat these problems and find serenity and fulfillment in your life.

In the next chapter, people with AD/HD who also overindulge or are addicted tell you their stories. You may relate to some of these stories and find them painfully familiar. By reading them, I hope you'll better understand how AD/HD contributes to overindulging in substances and behaviors, and be able to look at your own life with compassion, acceptance, and a willingness to get help.

THE MISSING PUZZLE PIECE

stories
of
AD/HD
and
addiction

DID YOU STRUGGLE IN school because you got bored or had a hard time paying attention? Was it hard for you to control yourself and act the way adults wanted you to act? As an adult, are relationships difficult for you? Do your impulses carry you from job to job, relationship to relationship, town to town, country to country, before you realize what you're doing? Are you ever distracted by the screeching of your mind as it skids to a stop when you're trying to recall a friend's name or your own address? Do you feel like you're working far below what you could or would like to be doing?

At one time I could answer yes to most of those questions. My life was run ragged by my untreated AD/HD. For years I tried to treat my AD/HD with alcohol and drugs. Now it's been many years since I've taken a drink or used drugs, and I don't think about them much anymore. They are no longer an option, because living in the solution to both my addictions and my AD/HD is an ongoing part of my life.

If you have AD/HD and have lost control over your eating, drug and alcohol use, or behavior, we both know how difficult and painful life can be. You, too, have experienced the shame and humiliation of being out of control. Your life has probably not been easy. In fact, it may have been a relentless series of struggles for as long as you can remember, at work, in school, in relationships, and with yourself. Your attempts to control your behavior are unsuccessful. Without help you fail, and failure is all too familiar to you. I know it was for me.

THE PUZZLE PIECES COME TOGETHER

I had been clean and sober for over a decade when I experienced a new rock bottom because of my AD/HD. Okay, I'm living a sober life and very involved in recovery programs, so why am I so disorganized and unable to cook dinner and carry on a conversation at the same time? Why do I have massive shame attacks when I realize that I totally dominated a conversation or blurted out an offensive joke at Christmas dinner? I'd had problems staying on track, finishing things, being easily bored, and not being able to contain my mental and physical restlessness for as long as I could remember.

I thought all of those problems would go away when I got sober, but instead they got worse. I was frustrated, because I knew I could do so much more if only I could pay better attention, follow through with my ideas, and focus my abundance of energy. Something was wrong. My willpower alone, which was tremendous, could not fix it. I was recovering from my addictions, but I had no idea that AD/HD was contributing to the ongoing problems in my life.

My experiences were not uncommon. Countless others have similar struggles, but at the time, I didn't realize this. I thought I was the only one with all these problems. Sometimes it helps to hear what other people are going through, to understand that we're not alone and that there is hope. So for the rest of this chapter, I'd like to tell you a few stories of people whose AD/HD threatened to destroy their lives. First up, Dana.

LIVING IN A FANTASY

Dana began creating and living in fantasy worlds as a little girl. She created worlds where she was beautiful, smart, and adored by others. Over the years Dana became a legend in her own mind. The fantasies she drifted into at home and during class protected her from the harshness of her reality. Dana had very few friends, did poorly in school, and was obsessed with being overweight.

Dana received passing grades in most classes, but her teachers and parents told her she could do better if she would only apply herself. Dana insisted she was applying herself. She was just forgetful, and her imagination was always traveling. Dana was intelligent, and in spite of her wandering mind, she graduated high school.

Dana was not impulsive. In fact, she took forever to make a decision. Even choosing her clothes for the day was next to impossible and often drove her to tears. Dana didn't cause trouble at home or at school, so no one ever bothered to find out why she appeared to be in another world, or why she was so lethargic. She didn't volunteer or participate in extracurricular activities, and everyone accepted that she was just a quiet, spacey, lovable airhead. Dana has what is known as AD/HD Primarily Inattentive Type.

Dana also had an eating disorder. She would take chips, several candy bars, and caffeinated soda to bed with her. Then, as she experienced the momentary pleasures of the sugar rush, she would fantasize about the life she wanted.

Dana never enjoyed drinking, because it made her feel even more out of control. One night she was introduced to a wonder drug: cocaine. This new substance did for her what food could not. The first time she snorted coke she had an "awakening." She felt as though someone had turned on her brain for the first time. Suddenly she felt alive. She instantly emerged from the trance in which she had been trapped for nineteen years. Dana could think. She could hold several ideas and thoughts at the same time. She had energy and felt the euphoria that cocaine seductively provides.

The second time she snorted cocaine, she locked herself in the bathroom at a party and read a book. Not only was she able to read while on cocaine, she could stay focused and enjoy the story without drifting into her own fantasies. Dana found herself using cocaine, when she could afford it, to read books, clean up her room, and pay her bills — tasks she was previously unable to complete.

Dana had a two-year love affair with cocaine. She moved in with a friend who was a cocaine dealer. At first the coke was free. Men were treating her to coke at parties, but eventually she was having sex with men so she could get loaded on coke. Then she was getting loaded on coke to have sex with men she didn't even like.

Dana lost weight. And as her use of cocaine continued, she lost control. Inevitably, she was arrested for possession of cocaine. Because she had no prior involvement with the law, she was sentenced to a drug treatment program. She was frightened and confused. How did a nice girl like her turn into an addict? She had lost all self-respect.

At age twenty-one Dana started a new life. She attended Cocaine Anonymous (CA) meetings regularly and worked the Twelve Steps of recovery. She was determined to stay away from coke and other drugs, and she did. However, she started over-eating again. She compensated for this shift in addictions with help from a therapist and Overeaters Anonymous (OA). But her self-image was shot. She was eating herself to death—and being eaten alive by her shame.

At twenty-three, with two years of recovery from cocaine addiction to her credit, she felt totally miserable and contemplated suicide. But instead of relapsing or killing herself, Dana went back into therapy. This time she was diagnosed as having biochemical depression and AD/HD. Because of her past substance abuse, Dana was extremely reluctant to take medication to treat her AD/HD and depression. She spent another year going to meetings, feeling miserable, and thinking of ways to end her life.

Her 12-step sponsor told her that she had to get professional help. As a last resort, Dana went back to the psychiatrist who had diagnosed her and agreed to try medication. Her doctor put her on an antidepressant. Within two months, Dana felt less depressed. But she was still not able to concentrate, focus, and read as well as she had hoped. Her doctor put her on a small dose of Ritalin, and Dana's ability to concentrate and follow through with things improved.

Dana, like others recovering from AD/HD and addictions, had to work very hard to maintain her recovery from cocaine and overeating. But now she had a chance. Now she was working with a brain that remembered, that could stay focused, that could help her think through the consequences of using drugs and eating sugar. Medication did not automatically take away Dana's low self-esteem, shame, and resentments. However, she now had the opportunity to work through her issues productively and create a better life.

Dana's journey illustrates one way AD/HD and addictions combine to wreak havoc with life. Next, I'd like you to meet Max.

MAD MAX SURRENDERS

While Max and Dana have very different lifestyles, they have a great deal in common. Max is a forty-four-year-old single man who has been divorced twice. He loves children, but felt he never had time to have any of his own. Max is a very successful real estate developer.

Max came to see me as a last resort because he had a plan to "blow his brains out." He was suicidal and angry. He had tried to get and stay sober for over twenty years. No matter how hard he tried, he was never able to put more than a year or two of continuous sobriety together. He had recently relapsed after eighteen months of recovery, and felt that he would never be able to stay sober.

At Max's first appointment, he started talking and didn't take a breath for forty minutes. He shifted from topic to topic and bombarded me with his anger and shards of information from all areas of his life. Fortunately my AD/HD brain followed him quite easily. The following is the condensed version of what he told me.

> I'd rather kill myself than live like this. Killing myself is the only thing I have control over. My life is a mess. I can't find anything. I have important contracts scattered all over my house. I'm late to everything. I make a lot of money, then I lose it. Money means nothing to me. I work all the time and don't finish anything. I have no time to enjoy my money. I'm always angry and I hate myself. My only friends are in AA, and now I'm drinking. I don't want them to see me like this again. I've been sober so many times. I don't know what happens to me. It's like my brain goes dead. I forget I'm an alcoholic, someone offers me a drink, and I take it. Next thing I know, months have passed, and my life and drinking are so bad that I go into another treatment program. I can't do this anymore.

After listening carefully, I asked Max how long he'd had problems finding things, getting to places on time, and finishing projects, and if he'd had problems in school. He told me that he was always in trouble for talking in class and fighting. He went on to say that he was a major disappointment to his father who was the superintendent of the school district. He then said something that many people with AD/HD say: "I was the kid with great potential, who never got good grades."

I asked Max if he really wanted to die or if he didn't want to keep living the way he was. He responded by saying that he didn't want to die, but knew he'd never get better. He'd been to the best treatment facilities and worked with the best doctors and therapists that money could buy.

I looked Max straight in the eyes and said, "Max, what if you have a condition that no one has diagnosed yet? And what if this condition contributes to your inability to stay sober?" He looked puzzled, but interested. I went on to say that although I couldn't diagnosis him in our short meeting, I suspected that he might have Attention-Deficit/Hyperactivity Disorder. Max smiled, and said that one of his high school teachers told his father he thought Max had AD/HD. "My old man said there was no way, that I just didn't try hard enough."

After talking more about symptoms of AD/HD and alcoholism, I asked Max if he would agree to not harm himself, try not to drink, and see me the next day. He agreed, and left the session with an appointment card, some information about AD/HD, and hope.

Max returned the next day sober and eager to find out more about adult AD/HD. After several sessions it became clear that Max did in fact have AD/HD (Primarily Combined Type). Just knowing that there is a name for some of the ways he thinks and acts was a huge relief for him.

Max agreed to attend AA meetings, not drink, and talk with his sponsor. He told me, "If this doesn't work, I'm still going to kill myself." He agreed to put the "kill myself" decision aside for ninety days and then evaluate his progress.

I referred Max to a psychiatrist who specializes in AD/HD and addiction. After much protesting, Max agreed to try a medication called Wellbutrin, which helped lift his depression and increase his ability to focus and concentrate. Before our ninety-day agreement was up, Max informed me that he was no longer suicidal. Ten months later, Max and his doctor talked about adding a stimulant drug called Adderall. The combination of Adderall, sobriety, and AD/HD treatment helped Max focus in ways that he never knew were possible. "Is this how normal people think and act?" he asked me. I smiled and told him, "I have no idea how normal people think and act, but I do know that you are sober, no longer suicidal, and making great changes in your life."

At the time of this writing, Max has five years of continuous sobriety, and is in what he describes as a healthy relationship. He attends several AA meetings a week and visits his psychiatrist every few months for medication monitoring. Max continues to work on his organization problems, his work addiction, and curbing his impulsive desires to jump from one business project to another.

DRIVING UNDER THE INFLUENCE OF AD/HD

Gracie is a forty-six-year-old woman who has never married. She has suffered from severe AD/HD since she was a girl, yet went undiagnosed until she was in her forties. Gracie has been in recovery from alcoholism for six years. Due to her history of addiction, she opted not to take medication for her AD/HD.

It was three in the morning. Gracie was exhausted from working a long shift as nursing assistant at the local hospital. Her cigarette hit the steering wheel as she turned onto the interstate and landed in her lap. The thought of pulling over to find the smoldering embers never occurred to her. Instead she did what many people with AD/HD would do: She continued driving while trying to extinguish the rolling cigarette butt. Ah! At last she was successful. She kept driving, oblivious to the lights and sirens of the highway patrol car that was following her. After a mile or two Gracie noticed the red lights, but assumed the officer was in pursuit of someone else and kept driving.

The officer pulled up next to Gracie and motioned her to pull over. *I wonder what he wants?* she thought as she turned down her Sheryl Crow CD and pulled to the side of the highway. As the already frustrated officer approached her car, Gracie hopped out. "Back in your car, ma'am," the officer ordered, his hand on his service revolver.

Gracie's anxiety skyrocketed as she realized there was a problem and she was somehow part of it. She became more anxious and confused as she tore her glove box apart looking for her registration. Gracie, like many with AD/HD, was talking to herself out loud as she processed where her papers might be. The officer then asked Gracie to step out of her vehicle, and asked, "Have you been drinking?"

Gracie, now agitated, began rambling at a manic pace about sobriety and rehab centers she was in years ago. When the officer asked her to recite the alphabet backwards her brain froze. The more frightened she became, the less able she was to explain herself. She became loud and belligerent. Like some with AD/HD, Gracie had poor balance and coordination. In her erratic state she was unable to walk in a straight line as requested. She failed the field sobriety test, was handcuffed, and taken to jail. It wasn't until hours later when the results of her blood test came back negative for drugs and alcohol that she was released.

It took months for Gracie to move through her anger, indignation, and humiliation. When she was able to look back at the situation, she realized that she didn't tell the officer that her erratic driving was due to a burning cigarette in her lap. She was also unable to express to the officer that not only had she not been drinking that night, she had not taken a drink or a drug in over six years.

Gracie gathered more information about people in recovery who take medication to treat their AD/HD. She and her doctor decided to start with the nonstimulant drug Wellbutrin. Gracie is a much more attentive driver and hasn't been stopped for a DUI since.

THERE IS HOPE

As you can see, there is no one poster person for AD/HD. Symptoms are expressed differently in each person at different times. They can be worsened by stress, environment, and the developmental stages of your life. The symptoms of AD/HD can have less impact on you when they are treated.

Not everyone who has Attention-Deficit/Hyperactivity Disorder uses food, alcohol, and other drugs to self-medicate AD/HD symptoms. Everyone with an addictive problem doesn't have AD/HD. It is estimated that 17 million Americans have Attention Deficit Disorder.[1] A review of the literature indicates that rates of alcoholism in adults with AD/HD range from 35 percent to 71 percent—a staggering number.[2] This doesn't include drug addiction or eating disorders. If you have AD/HD as well as an addiction, you are not alone.

The family I was born into is riddled with AD/HD and addictions. The family I helped create is riddled with AD/HD and recovery. It's never too late to start healing. The next generation will be even better prepared than we were to play the genetic cards they've been dealt. There's hope, not only for the next generation, but for all of us, right now.

HOW DO I KNOW IF I HAVE AD/HD?

checklists
for
AD/HD
traits

YOU MAY BE WONDERING if you or a loved one has AD/HD, or you may know for sure. If you've been diagnosed with AD/HD, allow yourself to skim or skip this chapter. If you've never had a clinical diagnosis but you suspect you may have AD/HD, stick with me. Because AD/HD is "normal behavior in the extreme," it's hard to tell if you have the actual disorder, or just AD/HD-like traits. If your symptoms don't impact you on a daily basis, it's not AD/HD. Let's talk clinical for a minute.

According to the DSM-IV-TR (the manual used by healthcare professionals to diagnose mental disorders), diagnosis of Attention-Deficit/Hyperactivity Disorder has three subtypes:

- *Predominantly Hyperactive-Impulsive Type.* This subtype consists of people who are more hyperactive and impulsive, and have fewer problems with their attention. This subtype is less common than the other two.
- *Predominantly Inattentive Type.* This subtype consists of people whose primary problems are with attention. They may or may not show some symptoms of hyperactivity and impulsiveness.
- *Combined Type.* People diagnosed with this subtype are hyperactive, impulsive, and inattentive.

For years the focus of treatment was geared toward helping children, and more recently adults, with issues of attention, impulsiveness, and hyperactivity. The creation of the Predominately Inattentive Type has expanded the diagnosis to include many adults and kids who aren't hyperactive, but who have trouble with listening, following instructions, organizing, and paying attention.

In this chapter, several checklists will help you assess yourself for AD/HD. While the checklists will probably be enlightening, they are not meant as a tool for self-diagnosis. Getting an accurate diagnosis from a professional with expertise and experience working with AD/HD in adults is essential.

You can answer the questions on the checklists yourself, but don't be afraid to get input from others who know you well. You will have opportunities to think back and remember AD/HD traits you had as a child and may still have as an adult. For questions about your childhood, try to contact relatives or close friends who can give you information you can't remember.

One major problem since the inception of the AD/HD diagnosis is that until recently, AD/HD has been viewed only in the context of childhood. Because professionals believed children outgrew AD/HD during puberty, adult AD/HD behavior and traits were given a wide variety of other inaccurate diagnoses, such as bipolar disorder, depression, and narcissistic personality disorder. As you will learn, it is possible to have AD/HD and other disorders. It's important to view AD/HD in the context of your lifelong development.

AD/HD IN CHILDREN

AD/HD traits can be present in toddlers, yet are usually diagnosed sometime between preschool and second grade. This is primarily due to the intellectual and social demands of elementary school, which require children to stay seated, to listen and follow instructions, and to learn reading, writing, and arithmetic. In the classroom, many children with AD/HD cannot compensate for their attention, impulse, and activity level differences the way they were able to before they entered school. At some point, these children realize they're different, and for them, different is bad.

Children also have to learn to wait when they enter school. They have to master waiting their turn, waiting to use the restroom, waiting for recess, waiting to eat, and waiting in lines.

Do you remember waiting in lines in elementary school? Many adults with AD/HD still haven't mastered waiting in lines. You can see them flip out at the Department of Motor Vehicles, IRS office, or supermarket. If you were one of those children who never mastered basic line-waiting, you know how hard school life was when you couldn't perform this "simple" task.

Success Deprivation

The self-esteem of young school-age children with AD/HD shrinks every day they're not treated. They feel awful about themselves and powerless to change their behavior. They don't understand why they're not like other kids and blame themselves for being stupid, lazy, hyper, and "bad." Unfortunately, too many teachers, therapists, doctors, neighbors, and family members blame these traits on poor parenting. Children with AD/HD are frequently viewed as misbehaving, undisciplined, lazy, or troublemakers who are victims of dysfunctional families. AD/HD can greatly contribute to family dysfunction, but dysfunctional families do not cause AD/HD.

School Daze

Kids with AD/HD can have an impossible time in kindergarten if they can't sit still, follow instructions, and refrain from distracting their classmates. Kids with moderate or severe AD/HD may be fortunate enough to be diagnosed and treated. However, others who aren't diagnosed will "fail" kindergarten or be passed on to the next teacher who may not have the knowledge or skills to help them.

Children with the inattentive type of AD/HD are less likely to be evaluated. They're not disorderly or disruptive. They usually daydream their way through school unnoticed. If you were one of these kids, you know what it's like to feel invisible. You may have studied two to three times longer and harder than your siblings or the other kids. You made up for what you couldn't learn by being quiet and good. You were your teachers' idea of the perfect student; they had no idea how hard you struggled and how much you suffered.

Don't be concerned if you can't answer all the questions or are unsure of your answer. It's best to put down your first response and not ponder each question for too long. The questions are divided into periods of human development: childhood, adolescence, and adulthood.

Rate each question with a 0 if it never applies to you, a 1 if it sometimes applies to you, a 2 if it frequently applies to you, and a 3 if it nearly always applies to you.

Questions About Childhood

0=never 1=sometimes 2=frequently 3=nearly always

_____ Did you have difficulty paying attention in school?

_____ Did you do poorly in classes when you weren't interested or didn't like the teacher?

_____ Were you easily bored?

_____ Were you forgetful, losing items such as books, homework, shoes, jackets, bikes?

_____ Were you able to focus intensely on subjects when you were interested?

_____ Did you daydream, fantasize, or act out during class?

_____ Do you think you got in trouble more than most kids?

_____ Were you the class clown?

_____ Did you feel awkward or less coordinated than your peers?

_____ Did you feel internally driven to move?

_____ Did riding your bike, skateboarding, ice skating, running, or swimming make you feel better?

_____ Did you spend hours in your own fantasy world?

AD/HD IN TEENS

For most of us, adolescence is the developmental stage in which we undergo tremendous change. Adolescence is the long hallway between childhood and adulthood. Teenagers tend to rush indecisively up and down that hallway, wanting to be treated like adults, yet acting at times like children.

Adolescence is a time of huge hormonal, physical, emotional, moral, and spiritual changes. Teenagers are bombarded by intense hormonal surges that change their bodies into replicas of adults. While they now have many of the physical characteristics of adults, they remain emotionally and psychologically immature. Adolescence is a critical and pivotal time in life where many begin self-medicating their untreated AD/HD.

Understanding how AD/HD and addictions affected you as an adolescent will help you today as an adult. Like most people with addictions, your emotional development may not have progressed much after you started self-medicating your pain, depression, shyness, anxiety, or AD/HD.

Questions About Adolescence
0=never 1=sometimes 2=frequently 3=nearly always

_____ Did it seem harder for you to do things that appeared easy for others?

_____ Did your daydreaming or fantasizing replace real-time relationships?

_____ Did you "zone out" when watching TV?

_____ Were you a risk taker or thrill seeker (driving fast, diving from high places)?

_____ Were you cited or arrested?

_____ Did you get traffic violations?

_____ Did you steal for the thrill of it?

_____ Did you drink alcohol or take other drugs such as marijuana, ecstasy, cocaine, speed, or heroin?

_____ Did your drinking or drug use get you into trouble?

_____ Did you ever think about killing yourself?

_____ Did you use reading as an escape?

_____ Were you clumsy?

_____ Did you feel uncoordinated?

_____ Was it hard for you to think through the consequences of your actions?

AD/HD IN ADULTHOOD

I've broken down the adult portion of this questionnaire into several categories. Each concentrates on a specific area of adult behavior. You will have the opportunity to answer questions about your attention, sensitivity, activity level, and impulsiveness. Don't worry if some questions seem contradictory. AD/HD manifests differently in each individual. For example: Some people can do several things at once, while others may have difficulty focusing on one task. The same individual may be able to multitask at work and have a hard time completing one task at home.

Attention
0=never 1=sometimes 2=frequently 3=nearly always

Distractable

_____ Are you easily distracted?

_____ Do you use TV, computer games, or the Internet as an escape?

_____ Do you find yourself gazing into the refrigerator until you get cold?

_____ Does your mind bounce from thought to thought?

_____ Can you do several things at the same time?

_____ Do you misplace your car keys or sunglasses, or your car in parking lots?

Overfocused

_____ Is it hard for you to be interrupted?

_____ Do you get so involved in an activity that you lose track of time?

_____ Is it hard for you to do more than one thing at a time?

_____ Do you lose track of what you are reading?

_____ Do you have difficulty switching from one project to another?

_____ Do you work well with details?

_____ Do you overlook details?

_____ Do you hold on to grudges and resentments?

_____ Do you debate and argue over details with others?

_____ Do you get bored, irritated, or tired when filling out questionnaires like this one?

Sensitivity

_____ Are you sensitive to bright or fluorescent lights?

_____ Are you distracted by noises that others don't seem to notice?

_____ Have you ever felt like leaving your items in the cart and fleeing a crowded grocery store?

_____ Do you cut the tags out of your clothing?

_____ Are there materials you can't stand to wear (such as polyester, wool, nylon)?

_____ Do the seams in your socks irritate you?

_____ Do you find yourself wanting to turn down the volume of the TV or radio?

_____ Do you tend to feel your feelings and the feelings of others intensely?

_____ Do you frequently feel the need to explain or defend yourself?

Activity Level

_____ Do you have an abundance of energy?

_____ Is it hard for you to relax and do nothing?

_____ Do you feel driven to do something, even when you're not sure what to do?

_____ Are you a fast talker?

_____ Do you shop as though you're on a supermarket sweepstakes?

_____ Is it hard for you to get up in the morning?

_____ Do you sleep through your alarm(s)?

_____ Is it hard for you to find your focus for the day?

_____ Do you doze in meetings, during movies, when reading, or during conversations?

Impulsiveness

____ Do you say things you later regret?

____ Do you interrupt others?

____ Do you blurt out answers before others finish their questions?

____ Do you lose control of your temper?

____ Are you impatient?

____ Have you abruptly changed relationships, jobs, or residences?

____ Have you told lies before you realized it?

____ Have you shoplifted, gambled, or spent money without thinking through the consequences?

____ Do you receive traffic violations?

____ Have you physically hurt people or damaged property when angry?

Now that you've finished this lengthy questionnaire, give yourself some time to review your answers. Be especially aware of the questions you answered with a 2 or 3 (often or nearly always). These are the places where your answers will give you information about how AD/HD may be affecting your life. The more 2 and 3 answers you have, the more likely it is that you should be evaluated for AD/HD. Again, this questionnaire is not a diagnostic tool; the questions are designed to help you think about specific AD/HD traits that may be affecting your life.

I'm not going to give you a specific "scoring guideline." This checklist is an opportunity for you to see your own behaviors more clearly. Almost everyone—AD/HD or not—will have many positive answers on this checklist. It's the amount of 2s and 3s that should raise a red flag for you.

After reflecting on your answers, you may be experiencing a wide variety of feelings. You may feel validation for what you already suspected or knew. You may be feeling relief, knowing that there is a name for what you have. You may feel relief learning that you don't have AD/HD. The title of Kate Kelly and Peggy Ramundo's groundbreaking book *You Mean I'm Not Lazy, Stupid or Crazy?* came from a teenager's response when he was told he had AD/HD.

Don't be surprised if you feel angry. You might feel let down by all those who misunderstood or abused you, the family members and teachers who didn't get you help. AD/HD is a disorder of lost opportunities. It's common to feel sadness and grief. You might be wondering, what if your AD/HD had been treated when you were young? How would your life be different? If only you hadn't overindulged or become addicted. I want you to know it's natural to feel the anger, loss, or grief, and there is hope for a better life. As you continue reading, you will find many solutions and strategies to treat your AD/HD, overindulging, and addiction. Never give up hope for yourself or someone you love.

FROM OVERINDULGING TO ADDICTION

4

evaluating
your
relationship
with
drugs
and
alcohol

TAKE A MOMENT AND picture an alcoholic and a drug addict. Do you see yourself, your partner, spouse, child, grandparent, or neighbor? Or do you see the outdated stereotype of a skid row bum, or a drunken woman picking up men in a bar? Alcoholics and addicts are parents, Girl Scout leaders, soccer coaches, dentists, teachers, bank tellers, executives, ministers, police officers, therapists, brick layers. There is no "classic" alcoholic or drug addict.

Look at yourself in the mirror. Could you be an alcoholic or drug addict? Do you think of yourself as a social drinker or someone who overindulges at times? Could you be dependent on alcohol or prescription or illegal drugs?

Your family, friends, and professionals may have their opinions about your relationship with drugs and alcohol, but in the end you are the only one who can honestly answer the question, "Am I using, overindulging, or addicted?" In this chapter, you will learn the characteristics of experimental use, social or recreational use, abuse, and addiction. You will hear stories from people who have been there. If your primary issues are with food, you will be able to evaluate them in chapter 10.

I struggled with these questions for longer than I care to admit. I'd like to spare you that struggle and help you get an accurate perspective on your involvement with substances. The purpose of this chapter is not to label you or make you feel bad about yourself. It is simply to help you take a closer look at your relationship with these substances. If you are already in recovery from substance abuse, you may wish to skim this chapter and move on to the next chapter about how people self-medicate their AD/HD.

In the previous chapter, you were given some tools to assess your own likelihood of having AD/HD. In this chapter, you have the opportunity to examine your involvement with substances and how they affect your life and the people around you. Part of determining if addiction is a problem is looking closely at your alcohol and drug use. First, let's look at five categories of involvement with substances.

CONTINUUM OF SUBSTANCE USE

When assessing your areas of possible substance abuse or addiction, it helps to use a continuum like the one below. Starting with abstinence, I will discuss each stage briefly, moving through experimental use, social use, abuse, and addiction.

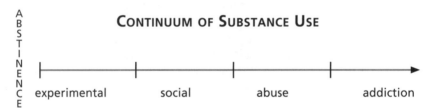

Abstinence
Abstinence means that you abstain, or do not use a substance. You may abstain from coffee, tobacco, cigarettes, sugar, alcohol, heroin, or other substances for short periods of time or for the rest of your life. Abstinence is a choice; even if you're locked up in prison you can get drugs if you want them.

Some people abstain for religious, cultural, or medical reasons. Others may have learned from the pain of loving someone who is addicted and have decided not to risk ending up on that path themselves. For some, abstinence is the only answer if they want to live. More and more, people are choosing to abstain from nicotine, alcohol, and drugs because they want to be healthier.

Experimentation
This means experimenting with alcohol or drugs once or twice to see how they affect you. Frequently, parents are convinced their ado-

lescent son or daughter is "experimenting" with drugs. When these parents describe several occasions when their children were under the influence and got themselves into trouble, they are describing drug abuse or possibly addiction, not experimentation.

There can be consequences to experimental use. Young people are especially vulnerable to losing control and getting hurt or getting in trouble the first time they experiment with a drug. This is especially true for adolescents and adults with AD/HD. The thrill-seeking behavior and impulsiveness of AD/HD combined with an inexperienced drug user can be a deadly combination.

Experimental use does not necessarily lead to serious consequences. Some people experiment, find out what it's like, and don't choose to repeat the experience.

Social and Recreational

Social drinkers and recreational users drink or use drugs at social occasions with other people. Their purpose is not to get drunk or high; rather it is to be social or celebrate at a wedding, graduation, or birthday party. They rarely lose control and do not undergo major personality changes. Social drinkers are the kind of people who may leave half a glass of beer or wine at the table when they finish their meal. They don't feel the need to finish it, because they're drinking alcohol as a beverage, not a drug.

A recreational drug user may take a hit or two off a marijuana joint every once in a while. This kind of person may smoke a cigarette now and again at a party and not feel any compulsion to smoke again. Their drug use is more about connecting with others and with themselves rather than disconnecting from themselves and others.

Social drinkers and recreational users don't experience blackouts, become violent or obnoxious, or try to seduce the bride or groom at the wedding. If a social drinker experiences a problem as a result of drinking too much, he or she will be cautious not to drink that much again. Social drinkers not only learn from their mistakes with alcohol, they are able to control themselves and not get into difficulties again.

Overindulging and Abuse

Overindulging is the same as abuse, which means trouble. You are not just drinking or taking a puff to celebrate at an event or social occasion. You are attempting to alter your thinking or feelings. You may be trying to numb your feelings, forget your pain, or feel better. People with untreated AD/HD are at high risk to want to do all of these things and may not have the impulse control necessary to regulate their intake and behavior.

With abuses come consequences. These can involve legal or financial issues, relationship troubles, problems at work or school, low self-esteem, and health difficulties. Some people abuse substances temporarily as a result of a life event or stressor. With minimal help they are able to abstain and even go back to true social drinking once they've worked through the situation that caused their pain, depression, or stress.

Many people like to think they've "only" abused substances and are not addicted. They hope to learn to control their substance use and become recreational users. Yet for some, this will be impossible. Some people are simply predisposed to addiction and lack the ability to drink or use drugs socially.

Addiction
Addiction and dependency are the same thing. Some prefer the phrase *chemical dependency*; others prefer *alcoholism* or *drug addiction*. Most recently, clinicians use the term "substance use disorder(s)." Whatever you call it, with addiction comes loss of control. If you lose control and cannot stop using despite the consequences in your life, you are addicted.

THE UNIQUE CHARACTERISTICS OF ADDICTION

Addiction differs from abuse in three ways. With addiction comes increases or decreases in tolerance; emotional or physical withdrawal; and obsessive thoughts and compulsive behaviors.

Tolerance
Drugs, including alcohol and nicotine, are substances that our bodies initially want to reject. For the most part, straight alcohol doesn't taste good. This is why many people combine hard liquor with sweet mixes. Makers of sweet fruit wines and wine coolers use a similar strategy with their products, which can be especially attractive to children and teenagers.

Many people report feeling nauseated and dizzy the first time they smoke a cigarette. In all these cases, the body's natural response to the toxin is to reject it. Yet the effects of alcohol, nicotine, and other drugs are so powerful and so attractive that some people will override the body's desire to rid itself of these toxic substances.

People don't consciously tell themselves that when they grow up they want to be an addict. Even with strong family histories of addiction, many deny they will become addicted. Most people begin by using substances to have a good time, to be like their peers, and to forget their problems.

Eventually, the user finds that it takes more drinks, pills, puffs, or lines to get high. When it takes more and more of the substance to obtain the desired effect, we say the person has developed a tolerance to the chemical. As substance abuse moves into addiction, people who have developed a tolerance must use more alcohol or drugs just to feel normal, and they no longer receive as much pleasure from the substance. Eventually, alcoholics and addicts experience withdrawal symptoms if they are not under the influence. At this point, they are compulsively using the substance to keep from experiencing withdrawal symptoms.

I've observed over the years that some people who are predisposed to addictions start out with a greater than average tolerance. These are the teenagers who out-drink their peers and end up driving their sick and passed-out friends home. Their tolerance will continue to increase over the years. At some point, depending on the health of their bodies, their tolerance may decrease. In the latter stages of addiction, people may snort very little cocaine, drink small amounts of alcohol, smoke less pot, and yet get very intoxicated, because their bodies can no longer process the toxin as well.

Withdrawal

When the addict's substance is taken away, he or she will go into withdrawal. Withdrawal symptoms are physically and emotionally painful, although they vary depending on the specific drug, the amount of the drug used, and the duration of use. It seems to be much harder for someone who has smoked two packs of cigarettes with a high nicotine content each day for thirty years to give up the addiction than for someone who has smoked half a pack of "light" cigarettes per day for a few years.

The physical withdrawal symptoms of most drugs pass within a few days to a week. Some drugs, such as marijuana and Valium, take longer to leave the system, causing a longer duration of withdrawal symptoms. Emotional and psychological craving can last long after the physical effects of withdrawal have passed.

Obsessive Thoughts and Compulsive Behaviors

With addiction comes obsessions and compulsions. I'm not talking about the clinical diagnosis of obsessive-compulsive disorder, rather a condition in which your attention is too focused or gets "stuck." John Ratey, MD, and Catherine Johnson, PhD, have coined the term "attention surplus disorder," and they use addiction as an example. "The addict spends his hours craving and consuming, and then craving and consuming again and then again, the drug (or activity—like compulsive gambling or shopping) that holds him in its grip."[1]

You find yourself constantly thinking about how and when you are going to get drugs or alcohol. This may mean going to a grocery or liquor store where people don't know you or meeting your connection. You can't stop thinking about using, no matter how hard you try. You have a powerful craving that becomes an obsession. The obsession drives you to do almost anything to stop the craving. The obsession becomes the setup for the compulsion.

The obsession is the thinking; the compulsion is the doing. The compulsion is eating the gallon of ice cream, snorting the coke, drinking until there is no more, gambling or spending yourself into debt. You have lost control of your thoughts and actions.

Now, take a moment, if you like, and go back to the Continuum of Substance Use on page 36. Mark with a pencil the spot where you fall on the continuum. You are the only one who can honestly place yourself.

IS YOUR SUBSTANCE USE CAUSING YOU PROBLEMS?

The following questions are not standardized research tools to give you a precise clinical evaluation of the effects of your use of substances; they are meant to help you evaluate your relationship with drugs and alcohol in general. I have divided the questions into six areas that substance use can affect: work or school, relationships, health, finances, the law, and self-esteem.

At Work or School

You may be someone whose substance use has not yet affected your job or schooling, or you may be painfully aware of how your career and education have suffered. Many people with addictions are able to hold themselves together during working hours and continue educational pursuits for a period of time. However, because addictions are progressive, it may be only a matter of time before your work is affected.

Answer the questions as honestly as you can by checking all boxes that are *yes* answers:

☐ Is your work or school performance suffering as a result of your substance use?

☐ Are you avoiding work or school because of your substance use?

☐ Have you received feedback from employers or coworkers who are concerned about your substance use?

☐ Do you feel that if you weren't using substances you could perform better at work or school?

☐ Do you live in fear of others finding out how much you drink or use drugs?

☐ Does your effectiveness decrease because you are hung over?

☐ Do you drink or use drugs before or during work or school?

☐ Have you dropped out of school or are you presently unemployed as a result of your substance use?

☐ Have you had an on-the-job injury while you were under the influence of substances?

☐ Have you been fired or asked to resign as a result of your substance use?

☐ Does your substance use affect your duties at home?

Your Relationships with Family, Friends, and Coworkers

When people become addicted to a substance, they develop a relationship with it. Their relationship with alcohol, pot, cocaine, nicotine, amphetamines, or narcotics becomes more important than their relationships with people. Nobody starts drinking or using drugs with the intention of neglecting their spouse, children, parents, and friends. However, addictions are so powerful that addicts frequently end up alone, feeling that their only friend is the substance that is actually harming them.

Addicts may be physically present but emotionally absent. They may be obsessed with thoughts about getting loaded, or engaged in behaviors necessary to get loaded; they may be under the influence, or experiencing hangovers and withdrawals. This doesn't leave much time to have relationships with people.

Please check all boxes that are *yes* answers:

☐ Does your drinking or drug use negatively affect your relationships?

☐ Do you avoid relationships that hinder your substance use?

☐ Do people in your life express their concern or anger about your use of substances?

☐ Do you put drugs and alcohol before your relationships?

☐ Do you sometimes forget conversations or actions?

☐ Do you engage in risky sexual behaviors while under the influence?

☐ Has your substance use cost you relationships?

☐ Do you argue and fight more when under the influence or when hung over?

☐ Is your parenting affected by your substance use?

What's Happening to Your Health?

Overindulging and addiction take a tremendous toll on your body. If you're young, you may not have yet experienced the damaging physical effects of addictions, which can range from weight gain or weight loss to diseases such as high blood pressure, liver disease, heart disease, and cancer.

Please check all boxes that are *yes* answers:

☐ Do you experience hangovers?

☐ Do you suffer from stomach problems, chronic headaches, shakiness, obesity, high blood pressure, or liver problems?

☐ Have medical professionals expressed concerns about your use of substances?

☐ Do you minimize or exclude information about the amount and frequency of your drug and alcohol use when talking with your doctor?

☐ Have you been putting off a physical exam for fear of learning the damage your use of drugs or alcohol has caused?

☐ Do you use drugs and alcohol to relieve anxiety, decrease stress, help you sleep, or decrease emotional or physical pain?

☐ Have you injured yourself while high or hung over?

☐ Have you been in a drug- or alcohol-related auto, work, or recreational accident?

☐ Do you smoke cigarettes or marijuana in spite of chronic bronchitis, emphysema, or other health problems?

☐ Have you been treated for drug (including nicotine) and alcohol related cancer or other diseases?

Money Troubles

Financial trouble can go hand in hand with overindulging and addictions, although not always. Some are able to stay afloat and can even be financially successful. However, many who are under the grips of addictions experience financial ruin, which not only affects them but their families as well. Most addictions are costly to maintain. Some people create debt so large they lose their homes and possessions.

Please check all boxes that are *yes* answers:

☐ Has your drinking or drug use cost you money in the form of fines, DUI classes, attorney fees, medical treatment, divorce, or business losses?

☐ Do you spend more of your income than you would like on drugs or alcohol?

☐ Have you borrowed money to buy drugs or alcohol?

☐ Have you compromised yourself or your values to obtain alcohol or drugs?

☐ Do you overspend or lose money when you are under the influence?

☐ Would you be in better financial shape if you didn't drink or use drugs?

Legal Problems

You may be the kind of alcoholic or addict who hasn't yet encountered the law. If you are, please don't use your "good luck" to deny that drugs and alcohol are creating problems in your life.

More common is the person who has been arrested for driving under the influence (DUI). As this occurrence has become more unacceptable, the penalties have become more expensive and more severe. Gone are the days of a warning and citation. You can go to jail for a DUI in some states, even if there was no accident and no injuries.

Klaus Miczek of Tufts University has said that "about 60 percent of all violent acts, whether murders, child abuse, family abuse, assault, or felonies, are associated with the consumption of alcohol."[2] These statistics do not include the consumption of drugs.

Please check all boxes that are *yes* answers:

☐ Have you ever been arrested for any alcohol or drug violation?

☐ Have you committed a crime while under the influence, including DUI?

☐ Have you committed crimes to pay for drugs or alcohol?

☐ Have you had legal problems because of poor judgment due to drinking and drug use?

☐ Do you put yourself at physical or legal risk in order to obtain drugs or alcohol?

☐ Are you doing anything in your life now that is illegal?

Self-Esteem: How Do You Feel About Yourself?

It's hard to feel good about yourself when you're out of control. Many people would rather feel shame, anger, guilt, self-loathing, or anything other than their own powerlessness to stop their addictions. Every day that you swear to yourself or to God that you won't drink or use drugs, and then you do, you feel worse about yourself. The vicious cycle of abstinence and relapse creates tremendous feelings of shame, depression, despair, and hopelessness. These powerful feelings have led some alcoholics and addicts to take their own lives.

Please check all boxes that are *yes* answers:

☐ Do you feel bad about your drug and alcohol use?

☐ Do you try to keep your use of substances a secret?

☐ Is it hard for you to forgive yourself for the ways you have treated others?

☐ Do you suffer from periods of self-loathing?

☐ Have you tried to stop drinking or using drugs, only to relapse?

☐ Have you ever felt demoralized or humiliated by your behavior while under the influence?

☐ Have you thought about or attempted suicide because of your substance use?

☐ Do you feel guilty if you lie about your drinking and drug use?

☐ Do you feel powerless to stop using drugs and alcohol?

> If substance use or compulsive behavior is affecting any of the following areas:
>
> - Work or school
> - Relationships
> - Health
> - Finances
> - The law
> - Self-esteem
>
> **THE BOTTOM LINE**
>
> and in spite of consequences you cannot stop, you have an addiction.

LOOK AT YOURSELF

Now that you've finished answering the questions, sit back and look at your "yes" answers. The more you have, the greater the chance that you have an addiction.

If you're not sure if you have an addiction, it's a good idea to talk with a professional who can help you look at your use in more detail. Some people need to keep abusing substances until it gets so bad they can no longer deny their problem.

However, you don't have to lose a relationship or job, hurt or kill someone while driving intoxicated, or humiliate yourself or your family in order to get help. You also don't have to live with the degradation and humiliation of your addictions. You can get help now.

The rest of this chapter will give you insight into how addictions develop and help you determine if you need to seek treatment. See if you recognize yourself or a loved one in any of the following categories.

Inability to Control Intake and Actions

Earlier we discussed the fact that AD/HD leads to loss of control over your attention, impulses, or activity level. The same is true with substance abuse and dependency. You lose the ability not only to control how much you drink or use, but how you act when you're under the influence.

No one starts out the day thinking, *Maybe I'll go out and get arrested for drunk driving tonight.* What happens is that some people start out drinking or using drugs to have a good time, relax, feel more social, or alter their feelings. In time, they lose control over how much they drink or use, and also over their impulses, behavior, and judgment. Once the substance is in their bodies, they can't stop using more.

How much and how often you drink alcohol, smoke pot, snort cocaine, take Vicodin, use Ecstasy, or smoke cigarettes will affect your health, relationships, and quality of life. You may be thinking, *But I don't use that often.* You can experience severe and staggering consequences from occasional use, especially if you lose control.

Do you become self-destructive or harm others with your words or actions? Have you ever quit smoking and later turned to a cigarette for consolation during a time of crisis, then you were unable to stop? This is loss of control. *Once you lose control over a substance, you will never regain it.* This is a hard piece of truth to swallow. Yet it is true. Once you lose control over a substance, you will never regain it. You may get away with it for a while, but eventually you will become consumed by your addiction.

Trauma and Stress

The amount of trauma and stress that people endure can contribute to their abuse of substances. Life is stressful. Life is especially stressful if you have AD/HD. Some people decrease stress by changing their way of life. They may take a less stressful job or move to a slower-paced town. Regardless of your attempts to lower your level of stress, you may still misuse substances as a way of coping with the stress of everyday living.

Ironically, some people with AD/HD become addicted to chaos and stress. Stress and turmoil can be stimulating to the AD/HD brain. Some even make a career out of their ability to hyper-focus under stress by becoming emergency medical personnel, firefighters, and police officers. If they haven't developed healthy outlets to relieve their stress, they may find themselves desperately self-medicating with substances and behaviors.

Trauma is another factor that can cause people to abuse

substances and become addicted to drugs, alcohol, food, and behaviors. This has been observed over the years with veterans of Vietnam, the Gulf War, and war in Iraq. Severely traumatized by their experiences, they also lived under constant stress. Many of these men and women came home with addictions and a disorder known as post-traumatic stress disorder (PTSD), a syndrome caused by being subjected to stress beyond the realm of normal human experience.

People with AD/HD often grow up in families where addiction, child abuse, family violence, and chaos can create severe trauma. When trauma isn't treated, people will often try to treat the symptoms themselves. You don't have to be a veteran to have been traumatized or have PTSD. It's understandable why some people try to self-medicate their PTSD symptoms with alcohol and drugs. It just doesn't work.

Do You Believe in Magic?

For some, that first encounter with alcohol and drugs was magical, even if they woke up in their own vomit. Something very "special" happens to alcoholics-in-the-making that doesn't happen to those who grow up to be social drinkers. Alcohol does something for them that makes it worth the pain they suffer just so they can drink again and again and again. Eventually, their bodies not only get used to the toxins that initially made them sick, they crave it.

As human beings we can abuse anything from ice cream to nicotine, but for now, when I say drugs, I mean alcohol, marijuana, cocaine, amphetamines, heroin, LSD, Ecstasy, nicotine, and caffeine. I am also referring to prescription narcotics such as Vicodin, Percocet, Talwin, codeine, Fiorinal, Demerol, OxyContin, and morphine, as well as tranquilizers like Valium, Xanax, and Ativan, and sleeping pills such as Ambien and Sonota. For the addict, these drugs seem to scratch an itch the non-addicted person doesn't even feel. A drug's ability to relieve emotional pain and create feelings of well-being becomes so powerful that the addict will risk everything to get it. And I do mean everything!

I frequently hear stories from adults in recovery who describe in graphic detail the first time they drank alcohol or took drugs. Some were small children who were sick, and their parents gave them a bit of whiskey with sugar to stop a cough, relieve a toothache, or help them sleep. This is not a recommended practice, but many children took their first drink from a parent or relative. I'm amazed at how vivid the memories of a first encounter with alcohol and drugs are for many people, even if the incident occurred forty years ago. They say things such as:

- For the first time in my life I felt calm.
- I had never felt so good before. I wanted more.
- I fell in love with how drugs and alcohol made me feel and spent the rest of my life trying to capture that feeling again.
- Cough syrup tasted awful, but it made me feel so wonderful that I tried to catch coughs from my brothers and sisters.
- My mind stopped chattering. It became quiet and so did I. It was magic.

Addicts and alcoholics can spend the rest of their lives desperately searching for that "magic." The feelings are never as good as the first few times. Eventually, using drugs and alcohol makes them feel worse. Yet some alcoholics and addicts chase the elusive magic up to and through the gates of insanity or death.

Denial

We tend to think of denial as a bad thing—the blinding force that prevents people from seeing the obvious. Denial, however, can be good. It keeps us from being constantly aware of the fragility of our lives. Denial provides us with the emotional buffer necessary to survive traumas. Without denial, we might suffer from disabling anxiety as a result of living in a world with nuclear weapons and highway snipers.

But too much of anything, no matter how essential for survival, can become destructive. Excess denial kills people every day by preventing them from getting the help they need. How many times have you heard someone say, *It's not that bad,* or *I'll get help later*? People die because they deny the seriousness of a medical condition, the danger of drinking and driving, their high blood pressure, or the fact that they are seriously overweight. Yes, excess denial causes tremendous human suffering and even death.

If you are in recovery from addictions, you know how powerful denial can be. The same denial that made it hard for you to accept your addiction may make it hard for you to accept your AD/HD and the need to have it treated.

If you are not in recovery from addictions, you may have read this chapter and still be in denial about the seriousness of your addictions. If this is the case, please read on, for you may see yourself in some of the stories in this book.

Other people in your life who may be suffering from addictions may not only be in denial of their problems but will deny that you have a problem. These "friends" and family members may tell you, "Don't be crazy. You don't have a problem. Look at me. I smoke pot more than you do, and I don't have a problem." These well-meaning people can't have a clear vantage point from which to view your life if their minds are clouded by their addictions. Unconsciously, they may not want to lose you as a drinking and using partner, because if you get clean and sober, you won't be hanging out with them and getting loaded. Even more important, if you honestly look at your addictions, they'll have to look at theirs. Ask yourself: Are you, or others around you, in denial?

Adding It Up

After reading this chapter, you still may not be sure if you have a problem, or you may be wondering if someone you love is addicted. Sometimes information needs to settle in for a while. You will have many opportunities while reading this book to develop a greater understanding about your relationship with alcohol, drugs, food, and behaviors. In the next chapter you will learn more about three of the core functions affected by AD/HD: impulse control, activity level, and attention. Thank you for keeping an open mind.

THE
BIG
THREE

impulse
control,
attention,
activity level

5

BY NOW, YOU'RE STARTING to get an idea of whether or not you or a loved one has AD/HD. If you do, you may have spent the greater part of your life feeling different or just plain wrong. You've heard other people's repeated judgments about you, and you've internalized them. You've started to say the same things to yourself that were said to you. *There you go again, you idiot. You're always late!* Sound familiar? *How many times will it take to learn to shut your mouth?* Your internal critic says brutal things to you that you'd never say to someone else.

In this chapter we'll take a detailed look at what are considered to be the core traits of AD/HD: impulsiveness, activity level differences, and attention difficulties. First, though, let's talk about what AD/HD really feels like.

FEELING DIFFERENT

Many people with AD/HD express "feeling different" as far back as they can remember. If you grew up in an AD/HD family and you have it yourself, you probably feel different than your friends. Living in an alcoholic family and becoming addicted yourself can also contribute to your feeling of being different. If members of your family (including yourself) have both AD/HD and addiction, your life has probably felt chaotic.

AD/HD is the feeling that you just don't get it, whatever it is.

You don't fit. You watch people express their feelings and you wonder what you feel. You may feel as though you're only going through the motions of being human because you don't feel connected with others. Talk about marching to the beat of a different drummer! Having AD/HD means you question your perceptions. You wonder why life seems so easy for others and is so hard for you.

Having AD/HD is different from having a genetic predisposition for addiction. You either have it or you don't. AD/HD, unlike addictions, doesn't need a trigger to begin. If you have it, you were most likely born with it and you will have it for the rest of your life. Environment and stress can increase or decrease symptoms, but not eliminate them. There are also degrees of AD/HD. Some are affected by it more than others.

Continuum of AD/HD Severity

no AD/HD   mild   moderate   severe AD/HD

Mild, Moderate, or Severe

Although it's an oversimplification to say that a person's AD/HD is mild, moderate, or severe (because of all the related problems that often accompany AD/HD), let's take a brief look at Lindsey, Maria, and Christov. Their stories will demonstrate how people with different degrees of AD/HD may be affected.

Lindsey is a high-functioning criminal defense attorney with "mild" AD/HD. She is eloquent in the courtroom and is known as an excellent attorney. She also has a reputation for being scattered and late, and for occasionally missing filing dates. Her clients love her because she is so attentive and supportive. Lindsey's greatest problems are in her personal relationships. She works seven days a week trying to keep up with her paperwork. Men in her life complain that she's mentally somewhere else when she finally finds the time to be with them. When they leave her, she doesn't understand why.

Maria has "moderate" AD/HD. She is an artist who owns a retail shop. She gets so caught up trying to balance her art and business that both are suffering. Maria is very trusting and has hired employees who have ripped her off. She's in trouble with the IRS for not filing or paying taxes for the last three years. Like Lindsey,

Maria also has serious relationship problems; she is currently getting a divorce from her fourth husband. She's so disorganized she can't put together a list of her assets for her divorce attorney.

Christov has "severe" AD/HD. He has spent the past year in prison for repeated impulse-related crimes. Christov didn't finish high school. He's intelligent, but the only skills he's developed so far all land him in jail. One night after drinking a "few" beers, Christov saw a black motorcycle and decided to take it for a ride. He didn't notice he was riding a Highway Patrol vehicle until the radio started talking to him. Christov doesn't do well within the structure of prison. He is constantly disciplined for not following the rules. Because Christov doesn't like spending time in solitary confinement, he tries desperately to comply with the rules, but he just can't pay attention and follow through, although he feels like he's trying as hard as he can.

These three examples provide some rough guidelines of how the degree and severity of AD/HD might affect a person's life. They don't give us an exact list of predictable behaviors for each level of AD/HD—of course, it isn't that simple. Each person is affected differently. All people with severe AD/HD do not end up in prison, just as all people with mild AD/HD do not fail in relationships.

What Does AD/HD Look and Feel Like?

If you have AD/HD, you don't always have control over your attention, emotions, or activity level. Interestingly, addictions are characterized by loss of control over some of these same functions. Loss of control over our neurochemistry creates different problems for each of us, but here are some areas that are commonly affected:

- Attention
- Frustration level
- Ability to follow through
- Activity level
- Impulse control
- Organization
- Memory
- Mood
- Rage
- Sensitivity
- Sleep
- Emotional availability

Problems in the preceding areas often lead to difficulties with the following:

- Relationships
- Work, school, and career opportunities
- Substance abuse and addiction
- Eating disorders
- Depression
- Accidents
- Encounters with the law
- Low self-worth
- Physical and emotional well-being
- Finances

Does any of this sound familiar? You may be thinking, "Yes, but doesn't everyone have some difficulty in these areas? Aren't these human problems we all have to deal with?"

The answer is yes! AD/HD involves normal human behaviors carried to the extreme. Sometimes even professionals have a hard time differentiating AD/HD traits from normal behaviors. Everyone forgets things now and again. Anyone can be distracted for a while. All of us have moments of impulsiveness. And many of us have high or low energy levels. None of these behaviors indicate AD/HD by themselves—but put several of them together in one person, crank up the intensity, and you may be looking at AD/HD.

AD/HD is riddled with paradoxes. A paradox occurs when two seemingly contradictory conditions exist at the same time. For example, we are ecstatically happy about our new baby, yet we erupt into tears when we hold her. People with AD/HD can be extremely active or relatively slow moving. Many people with AD/HD jump from one extreme to another. Here are a few of the many paradoxes of AD/HD:

- Oblivious to details/compulsive about details
- Highly talkative/says very little
- Aggressive/passive
- Memory for details from the past/forgets important things in present
- Disorganized/extremely organized
- Needs structure/hates structure
- Risk taker/takes few risks

- Outgoing/introspective
- High energy/low energy

A person with AD/HD can be highly focused one moment and completely unfocused the next. This person may take a huge risk one day and be very conservative the next. Some people with AD/HD are quite contained in one situation, and then become impulsive and boisterous in a similar situation. At dinner on Tuesday, Jack is calm, eating quietly with his family. On Wednesday, Jack talks incessantly through the meal, subjecting the family to a barrage of chatter about his day. No, Jack is not having a manic episode, it's just his AD/HD.

AD/HD cannot be narrowly defined because no one manifests it in exactly the same way as someone else. AD/HD is as diverse as personality. Some people may be outgoing, funny, assertive, and excitable, while others are shy, quiet, calm, and introspective. However, we can identify some core traits of most people with AD/HD. Let's look at the most common, beginning with attention problems.

ATTENTION DIFFERENCES

It's not that people with AD/HD have a deficit of attention. It's that they lack the ability to focus their attention. If you have AD/HD, you not only have periods of distraction, your life itself is distracting. For example, you may regularly be so lost in your thoughts that you miss your freeway exit by two miles, or you may go out to get your oil changed and come home having accomplished many errands but having completely forgotten about the oil change.

Pinball Thinking
Some people with AD/HD have minds that work like pinball machines. Lights flash. Bells ring. Buzzers buzz. The action is constant. One thought triggers another. A word from that thought sends the pinball racing back through the mazes of sights and sounds.

The person without pinball thinking may send a few balls into the machine, push the levers a few times, ring a few bells, flash some lights, and then the ball drops down into the slot. They've finished their thought or action. For the person with AD/HD, it's as though the brain can't stop pushing those pinball levers, and the balls, bells, and lights are constantly moving, ringing, and flashing. The more stimulated the brain gets, the more pinballing it wants to do.

Pinball thinking can be fun and entertaining, especially if there's someone to play with. Some people take drugs to experience what people with AD/HD get all the time. The problem is that it can't be turned off at will. This makes it next to impossible to think and communicate in a linear fashion.

Hyperfocusing

Distractibility is not the only attention problem a person with AD/HD might have. The opposite can happen. Do you ever get so focused on something that you lose track of time? Do important people in your life say, "Honey, do you realize you've been at the computer for three hours?" or something not as sweet, such as, "Get off that computer now! You care more about that machine than you do me."

Some people refer to this as hyperfocusing or overfocusing. Anthony experiences it as having his attention captured. He is locked up behind the bars of what he is doing at the moment. Nothing else matters. His attention is hijacked.

Many people with AD/HD describe periods when their attention becomes so engaged that they can't disengage. The results of having your total attention focused in one place can be awesome. It's amazing what some people with AD/HD create during these periods of absolute attention. However, this type of attention can take its toll in relationship problems, exhaustion, fatigue, and sometimes failing health. When your attention is captured, you are elsewhere, which means you are not where you are. Your children or spouse will be talking to you, but what they say doesn't register in your thoughts or feelings.

People who tend to become highly engaged in what they're doing can miss out on life. Over the years they can become isolated and lonely. They may lose their ability to relate with others and, as a result, seek out solitary activities. This can cause tremendous problems in relationships and families. Molly is a good example of this.

Molly is fifty-four years old and lives alone. Her children are grown and have their own lives. Molly's husband left ten years ago because he felt Molly could not be emotionally present in their relationship. She would disappear into her work or hobbies and not emerge for days. Their lives became separate, and so they separated for good.

Molly was a very successful interior decorator. She worked constantly, even though it was not financially necessary. After years of her family begging her not to work so much, Molly sold her business. She felt that the only way she could stop focusing so hard on her business was to be completely divorced from it. Molly mourned the loss of her business and soon became a compulsive exerciser. She worked out at the gym and ran ten miles daily.

Molly came in for therapy after tearing her Achilles tendon for the third time. Her doctor told her that she must stop running and working out long enough for the tear to heal or she may lose her ability to walk for a very long time. Molly became very depressed when she realized that in spite of the severe consequences, she couldn't stop exercising.

This type of hyperfocusing can contribute to behavioral addictions—just one more way AD/HD and addictions overlap.

IMPULSES ON THE RUN

Impulsiveness expresses itself in two forms—actions and words. The AD/HD brain sometimes lacks the ability to think through all the consequences of words and actions. You jokingly tell the boss that the new manager reminds you of the green lizard in the TV commercials—an example of how you may be offensive instead of funny. While never intending to hurt anyone, your mouth just keeps on flapping. Sometimes you are painfully aware of what you just said, other times you don't notice. If you have AD/HD impulsiveness, saying you're sorry has probably become a knee-jerk reaction.

You may interrupt others. Your mind hears part of what they're saying and immediately responds with your thoughts. Meanwhile, you've cut off the person who was talking and may not even realize you've done it. You may also have a hard time monitoring how much you talk. You give a five-minute answer to a question, when one word would have sufficed. Or you give expansive answers to questions that haven't even been asked. The information may be brilliant, but your listener is overwhelmed.

You may also impulsively over-expose yourself, embarrassing yourself by saying more than you really want to. Have you ever told the checker at the grocery store about the intimacies of your personal life? Verbal impulsiveness can be the equivalent of constantly living with your foot in your mouth.

Impulsiveness of action is also common. The level of reckless behavior can range from impulse buying at the checkout stand, to a spur-of-the-moment elopement, to criminal behavior. You might get a sudden inspiration and give notice on your apartment with no idea where you are going to move. You might like that new swim suit—and even be able to afford it—yet you steal it. I know a woman who stopped taking her AD/HD medication while on vacation and bought a timeshare. Fortunately, the contract contained a seven-day grace period and she was able to change her mind!

I have heard many tales of rash relationship decisions from people with AD/HD. Jean, whose AD/HD was untreated, lived in San Francisco. She had been sober for several years when she met Jerry at an Alcoholics Anonymous convention. They had a good time at the conference and he said he liked kids. Jerry invited her to come live with him. Four days later she and her daughter were traveling across the country in a U-Haul truck bound for Miami. Jerry turned out to be unemployed, not so fond of children, and physically abusive. Jean packed up her daughter and headed back to California, but stopped in Alabama to visit relatives and decided to stay. She got a job and an apartment, and eventually got her AD/HD treated.

DIFFERENCES IN ACTIVITY LEVEL

Do you have enough energy to power the Boston subway system? Are you a fast thinker and an even faster talker? Do you ricochet from project to project? Many people with AD/HD have an abundance of energy yet lack the ability to focus it in the direction they desire. If you are a toe-tapping, leg-bouncing, nail-biting pacer, you know how uncomfortable this energy feels.

A Restless Body

Some people with AD/HD need to move in order to think. There is a connection between moving their body and their ability to organize thoughts. I refer to this as a Cognitive-Kinesthetic Connection. A child with AD/HD may move around the classroom because it helps her focus. This behavior is usually distracting to the other students, especially in a classroom of thirty or more children. So the child is told to sit still. And when she does, her brain shuts down. She can't think unless she is moving.

Some people who *don't* have AD/HD think better while moving. Often referred to as Kinesthetic or Tactile Learners, these people learn best when they're involved in an active, hands-on way. This, in itself, is a learning style, not an indicator of AD/HD.

If this child manages to get an education (which is difficult with untreated AD/HD), she may choose a career that requires movement. She may use her body by doing physical work or become a teacher who thinks on her feet. She may become a park ranger, or a trial attorney who is able to move about as she speaks. However, not everyone with AD/HD is fortunate enough to find a suitable career. Some cling to the traditional belief that sitting still is important, even if they have to use alcohol or drugs to keep themselves in their chairs.

These children and adults suffer from extreme physical restlessness. Their bodies crave constant motion. It's physically painful to be still for long, and "long" may only be a few minutes. If you have a sedentary career, you may feel like there are shackles on your ankles and wrists.

You may run, swim, or work out during lunch or after work, but it may not be enough to dissipate your energy, frustration, and anger for having to function in ways that are in conflict with your physical being. You've been this way all your life and may have accepted that there's something "wrong" with you. Other adults seem able to sit still. I heard a teenager put it so well: "If you think it's a drag being around me, try being me."

You come home from school or work and find ways to calm yourself. You may start out as a child by using food and eat your way into a state of oblivion. When you're an adolescent, the world of cigarettes, alcohol, and drugs may open its doors. To your relief, it works. You may choose alcohol, pot, cocaine, nicotine, amphetamines, inhalants, tranquilizers, or heroin. You feel calmer, or your restlessness no longer bothers you. But it's only a matter of time until the solution becomes the problem.

A Restless Brain

Do you have a brain that's on the go day and night? Has sleeping always been difficult? Are you awakened by your brain's chattering before the sun comes up? Your restless brain may jump-start the second you become conscious, and off you go with incessant thoughts, dialogues, songs, new ideas, old ideas, memories, connections, disconnections, scenarios, and fantasies.

All of this brain activity can make it difficult to focus and follow through with things as simple as brushing your teeth. A restless brain comments on everything you think or do. It's as though a committee of diverse people all decided to yak at the same time. These "people" are loud, excitable, and rarely shut up. Your gray matter has the energy of a playful puppy trapped in the house on a rainy day.

Less Active AD/HD

You don't have to be hyperactive to have AD/HD. People with Primarily Inattentive Type have a "normal" to low activity level, and they are not impulsive. Their primary issues revolve around their inability to focus and sustain attention. This is especially true of girls and women.

Many professionals still believe AD/HD means hyperactivity, and don't recognize AD/HD when it only affects attention. People with inattentive AD/HD are frequently not diagnosed during childhood, because they don't fit the stereotype of a boy bouncing off the walls. Some with inattentive AD/HD think and move slowly. They can be intelligent, yet process information at different, generally slower, rates, so others view them as not being bright.

It's difficult for them to get out of bed and get going, even after several cups of strong coffee. Once they wake up, they have a hard time figuring out what to do next, and in extreme cases may spend their day trying to get started on something. This type of AD/HD can be painful and shameful, because our culture puts such high value on accomplishing as much as we can as fast as we can. It's hard to live life in the fast lane when you're running on empty.

If you have this type of AD/HD, you may feel like you live in a state of perpetual slow motion. You agonize so long over decisions, such as where to eat lunch, that lunch break is over before you've decided. It's difficult for you to start and complete school or work projects. You may have viewed yourself as lazy. For those with less active AD/HD, finding something good about themselves is sometimes harder to do than finding parking at the mall during the holiday season.

Frequently those with AD/HD Primarily Inattentive Type are diagnosed with depression, which they may also have. Antidepressant medications, especially those that work with serotonin only, will treat their depression but do not adequately treat their AD/HD. I have witnessed dramatic changes in people when their inattentive AD/HD is treated with stimulant medication.

THE HIDDEN DISABILITY

If you were born with a deformed leg or suffered from polio as a child, nobody would expect you to run the track like other kids. But AD/HD is a hidden disability. Your parents and teachers would not have been as hard on you if they had known. In our culture, if the cause of a problem isn't visible, the person with the problem may be blamed. Hopefully the information in this book will help you get the proper diagnosis and treatment, so you can stop living life feeling ashamed.

The AD/HD symptoms discussed in this chapter are the more common and recognizable ones. Yet there are quite a few other traits that are less common and therefore make diagnosis even more difficult. We'll talk about some of those in the next chapter.

THE LESS TALKED-ABOUT TRAITS

sensory
sensitivity,
sleep,
and
organization

DO THE TAGS IN your clothing or seams in your socks irritate you? Is it hard for you to get to sleep, stay asleep, and wake up in the morning? Do you worry that someday you may get lost in your clutter? If you relate to any of these questions, you may suffer from one or more of the less talked-about traits of AD/HD.

The purpose of this chapter is not to create a ruckus or controversy over changing the definition of AD/HD, but rather to discuss other symptoms such as sleep disturbances, sensory overload, and organizational difficulties as part of the AD/HD picture. Let's start by talking about sleep.

SLEEP

Getting a good night's sleep is a huge issue for many with AD/HD. They often report a history of sleep problems dating back to infancy and childhood. Brenda is a good example of this. "My parents would make me go to bed at 8:30 PM when I was in grade school, and I would still be awake when the Johnny Carson show came on at 11:30 PM." Brenda found out at an early age that cough medicine with Codeine helped her sleep, so she would fake coughing fits for a spoonful of the syrup. In adolescence, Brenda found that pot and alcohol would provide her with relief from her lonely insomnia. Waking up in the morning was always a daunting task even into adulthood. During college she was unable to take early morning classes until she started snorting cocaine. The combination of coke in the morning and alcohol at night ended her college career.

Brenda drank nightly for the next eighteen years. Finally, sleep was not a problem. But inevitably, the alcohol stopped working. Brenda could drink herself to sleep, but would awaken after three or four hours. No matter how hard she tried, Brenda could not drink enough alcohol to sleep through the night.

Brenda eventually got sober, but for the first five months of sobriety her insomnia was worse than ever. A doctor with experience in both AD/HD and addiction finally diagnosed Brenda with AD/HD Primarily Inattentive Type. With two medications, both her AD/HD and sleep disturbance were vastly improved.

Not everyone with sleep problems has AD/HD, yet many who have AD/HD have difficulty sleeping. Like Brenda, many find that self-medicating with food, alcohol, and drugs helps them get to sleep and stay asleep.

Most research on AD/HD and sleep has been done with children, and at the time of this writing, there are few studies with adult subjects. Most research on children has focused on stimulant medication as the cause of sleep difficulties. Stimulant medication can make it difficult for some to fall asleep, a side effect usually mitigated by decreasing the medication dose, or taking it earlier in the day. Ironically, some people with AD/HD take stimulant medication before bedtime. This enables their restless brains and bodies to slow down enough to get to sleep, stay asleep, and wake up easier in the morning.

Healthy sleeping patterns are essential for everyone, but especially for those with AD/HD. Here are some of the areas of sleep affected by AD/HD.

Difficulty Falling Asleep

William Dodson, MD, a pioneer of sleep research on adults with AD/HD, conducted a study of 327 adults with AD/HD. More than 70 percent reported not being able to shut off their minds so that they could fall asleep at night.[1]

Sometimes the AD/HD brain seems to wake up at nighttime or remain hyperactive twenty-four hours a day. Recognizing that this is a part of your AD/HD can motivate you to get help, rather than continue to suffer. It is also helpful for your friends, employers, and loved ones to know that your night-owl behavior is not intentional. The fortunate are able to find jobs or create businesses where they work and sleep at the most optimal times for their bodies and brains. Most people, however, are not so lucky. Being awake at night and sleeping during the day can be socially isolating and contribute to depression, relationship problems, or lack of relationships altogether.

Do you feel like you get your most restful sleep between 4 AM and noon? This sleep pattern is called Delayed Sleep Phase Syndrome (DSPS). While researching DSPS, Myron Brenner noted that a high proportion of individuals with this particular sleep disorder also had AD/HD.[2] This brings up the question, "Do people with AD/HD have sleep disorders, or are sleep disorders a component of AD/HD?" More research on the sleep problems of adults with AD/HD is needed to provide an answer.

Sometimes, knowing that what you are experiencing is real and happens to others can provide some peace of mind. Taking action with some new strategies may help you fall asleep:

- Set an alarm or several alarms to remind you it's time to go to bed.
- If you take medication to help you sleep, set an alarm to remind yourself to take it.
- Try to adhere to a consistent bedtime that is realistic for you.
- Try not to start exciting projects in the evening.
- Do something nonstimulating like paying bills or watching TV infomercials before bedtime.
- Listen to meditation or calming tapes.
- Try not to let your anxiety about getting to sleep keep you awake.

Problems Waking Up

Some people with AD/HD sleep so soundly they need several alarms to wake up. I know a man who sets three alarms three minutes apart. His final alarm sounds like a bugle and he has to get out of bed to turn it off. He has created a functional alarm system to get himself up, but it still takes him two hours to eat, get dressed, and feel alert enough to start the day.

It doesn't take a rocket scientist to understand why some people with AD/HD have a hard time waking up. When you don't get a good night's sleep to begin with, opening those ten-pound eyelids and keeping them open can be exhausting. Difficulties jump-starting your brain in the morning may date back as long as you can remember. You may also have a keen memory of all the "helpful" things that were said to help you get up. So on top of the ten-pound eyelids, you have fifty pounds of shame, all of which need to get out of bed. What's a person to do? Here are some suggestions if you take AD/HD medication:

- Put your medication and a glass of water by your bed at night.
- Set your alarm an hour before you have to get up, and take your medication an hour before you get out of bed.
- Have another alarm set to wake you up if you fall back to sleep.
- If this is too complicated, start by putting your medication by your bed. We're working on progress, not perfection.

Falling Asleep When You Should Be Awake

On the other hand, some with AD/HD have problems staying awake. They may find themselves yawning while a friend is telling them a story. They don't mean to be rude, but can appear that way, which contributes to more social misunderstandings. At work or school, they may put their heads on their desks when attempting tasks they find boring. Feelings of fatigue can occur even when they are well rested. This AD/HD brain demands a certain level of novelty and stimuli to keep it awake.

For some, physical movement can activate their brain. As discussed in chapter 5, some people think better when they are literally on their feet. They pace when they talk on the phone, brainstorm ideas, or need to concentrate. Unfortunately, social restraints can make it harder for these people to stay awake, focus their attention, concentrate, and be creative.

- If you take an afternoon dose of medication, set an alarm on your watch and/or reminder on your computer, and have your medication with you.
- Allow yourself to move around if it helps you stay awake and concentrate.
- Aerobic exercise increases levels of dopamine, norepinephrine, and serotonin, so try to incorporate it into your day.
- Take breaks, go outside, get some fresh air. A five minute walk around the building can make a world of difference.

What to Do About Sleep Problems

If the self-help remedies mentioned here aren't sufficient to deal with your sleep difficulties, find a physician who has expertise in AD/HD and addiction. When discussing your sleep situation, be sure to tell your doctor if you have a history of drug and alcohol abuse or addiction. Your doctor may suggest a nonaddicting medication to help you sleep.

If you have a history of addiction, it is especially important to be cautious or completely avoid medications from the benzodiazapine family (including Valium, Librium, Xanax, and Ativan) and sleep medications (Ambien and Sonata). All of these medications were brought on the market as nonaddicting medications, only to find that they have a potential for abuse and addiction. In addition, you will most likely build a tolerance to them quickly, and they are not helpful for ongoing sleep problems.

Make sure you trust your physician and you can talk to him or her about your medication concerns. If you are only offered "sleeping pills" with no discussion of your options or unique considerations, you might want to find another doctor.

Now that we've talked about sleep, let's move on to sensory overload—another problem for many with AD/HD.

SENSORY OVERLOAD

Having AD/HD can be like living in a house with window screens that have extra large holes. It's impossible to let fresh air in, yet keep out mosquitoes, moths, and dive-bombing blue jays. The AD/HD brain can be flooded by input and is sometimes unable to select what comes through its screen. This can lead to distractions as well as heightened sensitivity to sights, sounds, touch, and feelings. When too many stimuli come in from too many directions, there is no way to screen the significant from the trivial.

No wonder so many people with AD/HD have spontaneous rage attacks; their peace of mind is intruded upon by the ticking of someone's watch, the television program as they walk through a room, or the conversation in the next booth at a restaurant. They are irritated by the tags in their clothes and the seams in their socks.

People with AD/HD are sometimes too distracted to process information. Their minds work so fast that information doesn't have time to find a place to settle before more information jumps through the window. Memory is sporadic. You may be constantly bombarded with input that others may not even notice.

Enhanced Sensitivity

Has anyone ever accused you of being too sensitive or taking things too seriously? You don't have to have AD/HD to have highly developed senses; some people are just more sensitive to sights, sounds, smells, touch, motion, and emotions. My friend Eric can comfortably pick up hot objects that would burn my hands. Some people are oblivious to the sound of a car alarm, while others feel anxious and agitated until it stops. Our individual perceptions of sensation can be on a continuum ranging from low sensitivity to high sensitivity. For example, an autistic person may have very low sensitivity to pain, and very high sensitivity to sounds.

Heightened sensitivity seems especially common for many people with AD/HD. They may experience their senses with more intensity than others. Having highly developed senses can be a tremendous asset, but it can also interfere with daily functioning.

Sharon Heller, PhD, describes the problems and suggests solutions for what she refers to as "sensory defensiveness" in her book, *Too Loud, Too Bright, Too Fast, Too Tight: What to Do If You Are Sensory Defensive in an Overstimulating World.* Sensory defensiveness is a cluster of adverse symptoms that occur when a person is exposed to stimuli that most others neither find alarming or irritating. Dr. Heller states, "As many as 15% of otherwise normal adults have a nervous system that is overly sensitive to sensation."

A day in the life of sensory-defensive people is filled with noises that are too loud, lights that are too bright, smells that can be nauseating, and contact with fabric that is intolerably irritating. They may not be able to control their feelings of being hot or cold, and the touch of someone's hand on their forearm feels like being rubbed with sandpaper. Surprisingly, Dr. Heller states, "In fact, many AD/HD sufferers are sensory-defensive."[3]

What to Do

If this is you, make a commitment to take care of yourself with regard to your sensitivities. Become aware of sensations that irritate you. Stop judging, shaming, and comparing yourself to others, and start looking for ways to adapt your environment to meet your needs. For the situations you cannot change, look at how you can better adapt to them. Be willing to invest some time and money to increase your comfort. It is amazing the difference that fifty-cent earplugs, a twenty-dollar desk lamp, or a fifteen-dollar black-out shade can make. Here are some ideas for adapting to visual, auditory, and kinesthetic sensations.

Visual Sensitivity

Create lighting that works for you. You might want to darken a room, add or change lighting in others. Find ways to bring in more natural light, from opening drapes to adding a skylight. Most people find lamps more comfortable than overhead florescent lights. Have you noticed the humming sound florescent lights make? If the florescent lights at the grocery store bother you, try wearing sunglasses or a cap with a brim when shopping.

If you have a visceral reaction to clutter, invest time (and even money) in learning how to stay organized. The sight of clutter can literally make some people sick. We'll be talking about organization in the next section.

Auditory Sensitivity

If household noise, such as the TV or music, bothers you, explain the problem to your family or housemates and solicit their help in controlling volume levels. Have a quiet place you can retreat to. You may have to negotiate with those you live with for specified quiet times. If "white noise" is helpful to drown out other distracting sounds, you might invest forty dollars for a babbling fountain in your room. Of course, you could spend a lot more to replace your windows with double pane glass or install a solid-core door or other types of soundproofing. Do whatever you can, according to your means, to make your environment livable.

Consider wearing earplugs at movies, concerts, malls, or other places where sound is too loud for you. Ask friends to turn down or turn off the radio when riding in the car. It can be painful and exhausting to carry on a conversation when there is background music. Most people are happy to oblige after a brief explanation.

Kinesthetic Sensitivity

My friend Bruce used to say, "Style is dead, comfort is king." Allow yourself to put your comfort first. Cut those annoying tags out of your clothing, wear seamless socks, choose fabrics that are soothing. Don't wear shoes that hurt your feet or shirt collars that scrunch your Adam's apple, even if they are in style. Find ways to dress that are appropriate yet don't distract you. Consider getting a massage, taking a Jacuzzi, relaxing in a shower or bath if it is comforting.

ORGANIZATION

Getting and staying organized seems to be a lifelong struggle for many, but especially for those with AD/HD. It's amazing how some folks with AD/HD can have piles of stuff everywhere. They may even have a bike or vacuum cleaner in the middle of their living room. The bicycle in your living room bothers you at first, but after a while you no longer notice it. It may become a place to hang jackets and other clothing.

The inability to stay organized creates huge feelings of frustration and shame. Of all the AD/HD symptoms, organization doesn't seem to be helped as much by medication. Even with optimal medication, counseling, and coaching, staying organized can be impossible without help from others.

As with most things, organization is on a continuum. You may live with piles in certain areas of your home and office. Or you may live in such chaos that you cannot have visitors in your home. Organization problems are made worse when compulsive hoarding is involved.

Compulsive Hoarding

Most people with AD/HD are not compulsive hoarders. In order to meet the criteria of "compulsive hoarding" one must have so much clutter that areas of their homes cannot be used as they were intended. Compulsive hoarders frequently cannot sleep in their beds, eat at their kitchen table, or use their stove because of the stuff that resides there.

Those with hoarding problems may save the box from every small appliance, pair of shoes, or gift they've received. They may have old newspapers piled as high as their heads. If you or someone you care about is a compulsive hoarder, they will need more help than this book can provide. Find a professional who specializes in obsessive-compulsive disorder.

Help!

If you have tried to get your life organized without success, recognize that you need help. Your brain just isn't programmed to organize. There are many people whose brains can organize anything and everything. (They actually enjoy it—hard to believe, I know.) You may have a family member or friend who can be helpful. Sometimes just having someone with you as you go through things can help you stay on task. But don't ask a partner, spouse, or family member who will be judgmental or critical of you.

I've had both wonderful and horrible experiences with professional organizers (POs). One of the first POs I used shamed me for being so disorganized. I remember thinking, *Hey, if I had any clue how to do this, I wouldn't need you.* An hour later I realized I didn't need her. I paid her for her time and thought, *Don't let the door hit you on the way out!*

After that I knew I needed help from someone who would understand how my brain works and be willing to work with me. I have had the pleasure of working with organizers in my home and business who have been compassionate, understanding, and invaluable.

Professional organizers can change your life by helping you develop systems that work. There is no one "right" way to organize. It's important that you help create the system.

Paper, Paper, Paper!

Do you have paper, junk mail, magazines, bills . . . that seem to reproduce like mice? The first line of defense is to keep it out of your house. Look at the magazines you subscribe to. Then ask yourself: Do I read them or do they end up in the "wanna be read" piles? Be mindful of what you renew. You are paying for these potential pile builders.

Next, find ways to stop junk mail. Do an Internet search on "stop junk mail," and you'll find some helpful suggestions. There are websites that, for a fee, will send you pre-addressed post cards. All you have to do is fill them out and send them to the agencies that will take you off mailing lists.

Finding Misplaced Items

Do you lose things all the time? Usually the item isn't lost, it just can't easily be found. The answer is to have a system of organization that works for you, so that you can maintain it. Get help to create a custom organizational system for your home, garage, and office. You may never become an alphabetical order-file person who knows exactly where everything is. Progress, for you, may be having fewer piles in fewer places, thus limiting the square footage you will have to sort through to find that tax extension form. (Notice we are not even talking about making the April 15 deadline yet. One thing at a time.) Here are some tips for finding what you want, when you want it.

- Have a specific place to leave your car keys when you come home—a hook on the wall or a dish on the countertop.
- Use sunglasses straps, keys that clip to your purse or belt, and fanny packs.
- Create a "priority" file or pile where you can see it.
- Avoid endless paper shuffling by dealing with paperwork as soon as it arrives. Stock up on envelopes and stamps to mail bills.
- Try using color-coded files. They work because you can see by glancing at the color which category you're looking for.
- Consider decreasing clutter by getting rid of things you really don't use or need. Try not to be impulsive when culling through your stuff.
- Keep all tax forms and receipts in a separate file, box, or large envelope.
- Get clothes, lunches, briefcases, backpacks, coats, and keys out the night before.
- Accept baby steps in your quest to get organized, and don't give up.

Organization and Timing

Like many people with AD/HD, you may have a very different experience of time than most people. You may get lost in time, or you may be overly optimistic about how much time it will take to get someplace or get projects done. You may think it will only take an hour to run several errands. Your brain doesn't even register traffic, or the fact that it's the day before Thanksgiving. It takes time to train your brain to think about external factors.

Mark is an example of someone who loses track of time. He has the habit of starting projects that "will only take a minute," while his family is waiting in the car to go for a hike or vacation. Meanwhile, his wife, Betty, heats up along with the car engine. When he finally reaches the car, Mark has no idea why Betty, who has been waiting in a hot car for ten minutes with bickering kids, snarls at him. Working from a different experience of time can cause major problems with your work, school, the mortgage company, and the IRS. Here are some suggestions that might be of help.

- Buy a watch with a timer that will beep hourly. There are also watches you can set to go off at specific times of the day to remind you to take medication, eat, or shift gears into another activity.

- If you work with computers, consider a program with an alarm to let you know how much time has passed.
- Try not to get too stimulated and engaged in the evenings if you plan to go to bed at a certain time.
- Use a calendar, appointment book, day planner, or PDA to remind yourself of appointments and deadlines.
- Before you start to do something, ask yourself, "Is it realistic to start this project now?"
- Set priorities and stick with them. For example, if your priority is to get to work on time, bypass cleaning the kitchen or watering the plants if you're already late.

I Can't Do This—Until I Do That

It can be so hard for some with AD/HD to get started on even the "simplest" things. The most frequent problem is that they tend to bind themselves with a type of thinking. It goes like this: "I can't do this . . . until I do that. And I can't do that . . . until I do this." For example, you want to go pick up something at the grocery store for lunch, but you're so hungry you can't go until you eat. Because there is nothing to eat in your house, you can't go to the grocery store. Many with AD/HD have internalized this type of thinking to the point that they are constantly stuck revolving in the circular diagram below.

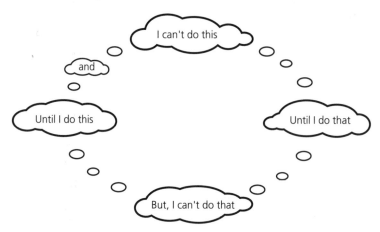

Moving out of this self-defeating thinking means being flexible to see other options. For example, you might be able to grab a sandwich or snack on the way to do your grocery shopping. Often this circular pattern is pervasive in the AD/HD person's life. It can affect every aspect of your life, and keep you from getting organized, starting home-improvement projects and exercise programs, and attaining careers and relationships.

Here are some suggestions to help you stop going around and around.

- Become aware of how you set yourself up to be immobilized.
- Look for ways to define your task differently.
- Ask for help from someone you trust—they may quickly see how you can accomplish your task.
- If you are stuck, do something, even if it is not the task at hand.

MOOD

Like many people with AD/HD, you may feel as if you're riding an endless roller coaster of mood swings. You may be powerless to control your ups and downs. Your mood may change dramatically from one day to the next or from moment to moment.

You may also suffer from volcanic eruptions of rage. You know your rage is much greater than the situation, but you can't seem to stop the lava once it starts flowing. Before you know it, you're standing knee-deep in molten rock, burning from the tremendous remorse and shame you feel about the devastation you've created.

In a short period of time your mood may reflect depression, irritability, anger, joy, excitability, and shame. You may have difficulty managing your impulses, which contributes to what may be perceived by others as irrational responses or changes in mood. You may find yourself confused and feeling awful about your responses and actions and yet feel powerless to control them.

Even though mood swings are common for people with AD/HD, it's important to rule out or treat co-occurring mood disorders such as depression and bipolar disorder. (For more information see the next chapter on co-occurring conditions.)

Here are some things you can do to balance your mood.

- Take two breaths before you act or speak (especially if you're angry).
- Remove yourself from the situation before or when you are angry.
- Become aware of what triggers mood changes.
- Before you make a major life change, discuss it with

trusted friends or a therapist, and be aware of the potential for mood fluctuation.

- Recognize when you start spiraling down the shame tube; you don't deserve to go there.
- Try not to get too hungry, angry, lonely, tired, excitable, or dehydrated.

I hope this chapter provided you with validation and suggestions that will help you with some of the less-talked about traits of AD/HD. Look for progress, not perfection. You won't be able to change your AD/HD behaviors overnight.

There are many things you can learn and change about yourself to make life with AD/HD easier for you and those around you. The first and maybe most difficult thing is to get off your own back. Stop blaming yourself for things that are beyond your control and start taking responsibility for things you can control.

GETTING THE RIGHT DIAGNOSIS

AD/HD
and
co-occurring
conditions

HOW DO YOU REALLY know if you or someone you love has AD/HD? If you used the checklists in chapter 3, you may be wondering how to get an accurate diagnosis. In this chapter we will discuss how to go about doing this. We will also discuss the importance of having all co-occurring conditions diagnosed. It is essential that everything that is going on with an individual is treated. It's not enough to treat AD/HD and leave a person with untreated depression, anxiety, eating disorders, substance use, or other disorders.

Even if you're convinced that you have AD/HD, it's important to be evaluated by a doctor, psychologist, or therapist who has a thorough knowledge of adult AD/HD. Don't rely on self-diagnosis. Even if you're a professional, let another professional give you an objective diagnosis.

AD/HD is a diagnosis fraught with questions and controversy. Many media sources express concern that AD/HD is over-diagnosed. In some cases, this is true. It is critically important that people suffering from anxiety, post-traumatic stress disorder, manic-depressive illness, personality disorders, thyroid imbalances, head injuries, and addictions not be diagnosed with AD/HD if they don't have it. However, people with AD/HD are likely to have other co-occurring conditions. In addition, some of the traits and symptoms of AD/HD mimic or overlap with those of other disorders.

As with any misdiagnosed condition, treating the wrong problem, or only part of the problem, can lead to serious consequences. Therefore, it's essential that AD/HD does not become the all-encompassing label we slap on adults and children who exhibit some of the symptoms. Each individual must be viewed in the context of his or her life. People in crisis or under stress can exhibit signs similar to AD/HD, but if these symptoms have not been present in some form during most of their lives, they are probably responding to their circumstances and don't have AD/HD.

On the other hand, many people who have AD/HD are not diagnosed. This is especially true of women, girls, and those who have AD/HD Primarily Inattentive Type.

When we talk about overdiagnosis or underdiagnosis, we are really talking about misdiagnosis. Educating yourself about AD/HD is your best defense. The more you know, the better health-care consumer you are.

While we are fortunate to have many fine professionals devoting time to one special illness or problem, including AD/HD, there is a downside to this specialization. An old saying goes something like this: "When all you have is a hammer, everything you see looks like a nail." For example, specialists who primarily treat survivors of sexual abuse might tend to see signs of sexual abuse in almost everyone they treat. I have worked with many patients who have received a different diagnosis from each specialist they have seen. Coincidentally, the diagnosis matched the practitioner's specialty.

HOW TO GET AN EVALUATION FOR AD/HD

The first step is to find a professional who has the experience and expertise to evaluate AD/HD in adults. Most treatment professionals are ethical and do not claim to specialize in areas where they don't have expertise. But unfortunately, some professionals advertise themselves as being experts in ailments that are more frequently diagnosed. Because AD/HD has become so high profile, AD/HD clinics and specialists are springing up all over. You want to look for a health-care provider who has had experience treating adults with AD/HD. It is also helpful if the professional you choose treats other conditions, and it's especially important to find someone who understands the interaction between AD/HD and self-medicating behaviors.

Finding the right person to evaluate you can be difficult. The best recommendations usually come from patients or former patients. Ask around, and you may hear the same names come up from different people. The last place to look is that full-page ad in the yellow pages or on billboards and shopping carts. Most clinicians who are exceptional do not have to advertise.

Before you make an appointment to see someone for an AD/HD evaluation or treatment, consider asking him or her the following questions:

- What are your credentials? (Only work with a professional who holds a valid license in his or her field.)
- How long have you been evaluating and treating adults with AD/HD?
- Do you also evaluate and treat co-occurring conditions such as eating disorders and substance and behavioral addictions?
- What do you think are important elements of AD/HD treatment? (You want to hear about AD/HD-focused therapy, AD/HD groups, coaching, help with organizing, and medication when warranted.)
- What is your fee for the evaluation and for regular sessions? (Fees vary according to geographic location and type of practitioner you see. However, it's important to know ahead of time how much you will be charged. It can take several sessions to make an AD/HD diagnosis.)

Lastly, only work with a professional who greets your questions positively and openly. You don't need to be treated by someone who is impatient or defensive.

What to Expect

Many professionals, myself included, use assessment tools (in the form of questionnaires) in combination with a detailed history to obtain an accurate diagnosis. There are several assessment tools that are reputable and reliable. I especially like the Brown AD/HD Scales, because they are available for young children, school-age children, adolescents, and adults. They are also reliable in assessing AD/HD Primarily Inattentive Type.

When your health professional is gathering a detailed history about you, it is important to collect information from other people in your life. Your spouse, parents, siblings, teachers, friends, boss, and coworkers can all lend valuable input. Look at school report cards, especially the teacher's comments where you might find comments such as: "disrupts class, doesn't sit still, daydreams in class," or my favorite, "not working up to her potential." Have someone else recollect details about you as a child.

Doctors Hallowell and Ratey, experts in diagnosing AD/HD, state in their book *Driven to Distraction*: "It is important to underline this point: the diagnosis of AD/HD is based first and foremost on the individual's history or life story. The most important step in determining whether one has AD/HD is sitting down and talking to somebody who is knowledgeable in the field."[1]

Diagnosing AD/HD is similar to diagnosing clinical depression. No blood test determines if your depression is primarily biological or reactive (caused by events in your life). Your doctor or therapist makes the determination by asking you about specific symptoms such as sleep and eating patterns, concentration, sexual drive, energy level, and ability to have fun. The diagnosis is made by looking at your family history of mood disorders, how you appear and act, and your description of how you feel and function now and in the past. Diagnosing AD/HD follows a similar pattern.

Other diagnostic tools can be used, including the T.O.V.A. (Test of Variables of Attention), a computerized performance test developed to assess AD/HD. Different experts will have preferred methods of diagnosing AD/HD. Be cautious of professionals who want to put you or your child through thousands of dollars of psychological testing, brain scans, or diet programs, unless you clearly understand why they need more information than what is provided by an assessment questionnaire and comprehensive history. This is not to say that if a professional asks for additional testing you should refuse. There are situations where AD/HD is one of many problems; in these cases, it may be essential to have testing for related learning disorders, allergies, and physical, neurological, and emotional problems. In most cases, however, a thorough history, with input from people in your life, should suffice for the initial diagnosis.

Recognizing Recovery-Based Symptoms

It can be complicated to diagnose AD/HD during early recovery from addiction. If you are self-medicating your AD/HD with drugs, food, alcohol, or compulsive behaviors, your AD/HD is being treated. It's not being treated in healthy ways or even in ways that work; nonetheless, you may experience some relief from your AD/HD symptoms.

When you become abstinent, which is essential for your recovery, your AD/HD symptoms may get worse as you are trying to get better. It is extremely frustrating when you're trying so hard to recover from your addictions and you're functioning and feeling worse.

The other confusing part about early addiction recovery is that many people without AD/HD will appear to have AD/HD during the first months of abstinence. They can be disorganized, restless, or unable to sit still; have difficulties concentrating and following through with commitments; and act impulsively. These AD/HD-like symptoms are common for some in early recovery. There are several differences between early recovery AD/HD-like symptoms and true AD/HD. First, the person without AD/HD will not have a history of attention, activity level, organization, sleep, or sensitivity problems that go back to childhood. The general rule for it to be true AD/HD is that symptoms must occur prior to age seven. (However, symptoms may not have been noticed at this young age, especially in those with above-average intelligence, women, girls, and those with inattentive type AD/HD.) AD/HD-like symptoms only appear when people get clean and sober. Second, these AD/HD-like symptoms go away within six months to a year. True AD/HD symptoms will not spontaneously disappear; instead, they often become more pronounced and more noticeable in recovery.

CO-OCCURRING CONDITIONS

When being assessed for AD/HD, it's important to tell your treatment professional about other symptoms or conditions you have. AD/HD is frequently accompanied by other conditions and problems. Few people with untreated AD/HD make it to adulthood without developing other problems, which complicate the AD/HD picture. Some co-occurring conditions are so interwoven into the fabric of the AD/HD experience that it is hard to separate them. Sleep disorders (as discussed in chapter 6) are a good example. Other conditions greatly overlap AD/HD symptoms, such as depression and anxiety, obsessive-compulsive disorder, and post-traumatic stress disorder. It's like sorting out and identifying all the colored threads in an ornate rug. Some are distinctly different, some have similarities, and others are so intertwined that they create new colors. Our best bet is to look at some of the thread of the fabric, without losing sight of the rug.

Here are some commonly co-occurring conditions that must also be diagnosed and treated.

- Learning disabilities
- Depression
- Bipolar disorder
- Anxiety disorder
- Obsessive-compulsive disorder
- Post-traumatic stress disorder
- Asberger's disorder
- Antisocial personality disorder

Learning Disabilities

Learning disabilities make it difficult to interpret, integrate, store, access, and express information. They affect other areas of learning, such as reading, writing, and the ability to express yourself with language. Because researchers believe that 40 to 80 percent of people with AD/HD also have learning disabilities, it's important to be evaluated for them under the following circumstances:

- You have a childhood history of learning problems.
- You have difficulty reading and writing.
- Your memory is impaired even when you're taking AD/HD medication.
- You consistently invert letters, numbers, and directions, and confuse right and left, clockwise and counterclockwise, and push and pull.
- It is hard for you to process information you hear, such as conversations or verbal directions.
- You have difficulty taking notes during meetings or classes and copying down information from the board.

Depression

Unfortunately, the English language uses the same word to describe anything from having a few hours of feeling "blue" to profound, immobilizing, psychotic, and suicidal depression. No wonder it's hard to determine if you are depressed or not. Sometimes people experience depression as a reaction to the loss of a loved one, a home, financial stability, or a job. Other times they suffer from depression that is primarily based in their biology. People with Inattentive AD/HD, especially women, are often misdiagnosed as being depressed. Overlapping symptoms include low energy, problems self-activating, poor concentration, memory impairment, and organization, as well as the inability to prioritize, set, and complete realistic goals.

For some, treating their AD/HD eliminates most, if not all of the symptoms of "depression." Others, however, continue to be depressed unless their depression is treated.

Bipolar Disorder

Bipolar disorder (formally known as manic-depression) is divided into two types. The primary difference between bipolar I and bipolar II is the intensity of the mood fluctuation and the resulting behavior. People with bipolar I have episodes of manic behavior that can include delusional, grandiose, and racing thoughts. They also experience an energy push that is either euphoric or agitated.

Those in a manic phase might buy an expensive car, home, or business that they can't afford. They may also stay up for days without sleep and exhibit accelerated talking, thinking, and activity that is off the scale of any AD/HD chart. For example, one man was driving by the airport on his way to a job interview when he was struck by a brilliant solution to his financial problems. He flew to Reno and gambled all of his savings in two days. His grandiose thinking convinced him that he would win enough to cover his losses and support his family in style.

The depressive episode is also severe. People with bipolar disorder can experience delusions, suicidal thoughts, and serious if not fatal suicide attempts.

Bipolar II is much easier to confuse with AD/HD. Those with bipolar II do not have classic manic episodes, yet the depression can be as severe.

Here are some of the places where bipolar and AD/HD overlap. People with both disorders can experience talkativeness, irritability, agitation, impulsivity, impatience, poor judgment, hyperactivity, restlessness, sleep problems, and hypersexuality. With this many overlapping symptoms, it is easy to understand how these disorders can be misdiagnosed.

If we take a closer look, you can also see the differences between the two:

- AD/HD symptoms impair your life daily. Bipolar symptoms happen in episodes that may be years apart.

- AD/HD mood fluctuations can occur in the same day or hour, and are problematic throughout the person's life. The manic high or depressed low of bipolar can last for weeks or months.
- People with AD/HD frequently have chronic sleep problems. Those with bipolar have episodes of reduced need to sleep, which usually lasts several days.
- AD/HD symptoms do not include psychotic thought disorder, while bipolar can.

Studies suggest that 20-25 percent of people with bipolar also have AD/HD.[2] Treatment is available for both conditions. Because bipolar is episodic, some with AD/HD don't realize that they have had a bipolar episode. Treating AD/HD with stimulant medication can, in some cases, trigger a manic episode. If you think you may have a history of bipolar, be sure to mention it to your doctor. He or she may begin your treatment by stabilizing your mood, then add medication to treat your AD/HD.

Anxiety Disorder

People with untreated AD/HD can appear anxious, just as those with anxiety disorders can seem like they have AD/HD. Some have both. Here are some of the places where anxiety disorders and AD/HD overlap: restlessness, edginess, difficulty concentrating, obsessive thinking, and sleep disturbances. When AD/HD is the primary problem, people usually feel less anxious as it is treated.

On the other hand, if the anxiety disorder is not related to AD/HD, it needs to be stabilized first. Otherwise, AD/HD medications can increase the person's anxiety.

Obsessive-Compulsive Disorder

In severe or "classic" cases of obsessive-compulsive disorder (OCD), sufferers will wash their hands until they are raw. Others have frightening and self-abusive thoughts that repeat like a broken record. Some are compelled to repeat rituals such as chewing their food eight times on each side of their mouth for fear that if they only chew seven times they will choke. If their chewing is interrupted they have to start over. Some with OCD are constantly tormented by their obsessive thoughts and are continually fighting to resist their compulsions (especially around others).

OCD has been brought to the public's attention through movies and television. Jack Nicholson's portrayal of Melvin Udall, in the film *As Good as It Gets*, shows some of the daily struggles and relationship problems people with OCD experience. In the movie *Matchstick Men*, Nicolas Cage plays con man Roy Waller who has OCD and Tourette's syndrome. These films give movie-goers some insights into living with OCD, although there is no way to portray the relentless, tedious, and fearful thoughts that loop through the brain of those with OCD. And there is nothing humorous about living with this disorder.

There are also those who do not meet the diagnostic criterion for OCD. Some people have what Daniel Amen, MD, refers to as the overfocused type of AD/HD. These people get stuck in negative thought patterns, have trouble seeing options, tend to overfocus on things that interest them, worry excessively, and get stuck carrying grudges. Those with the overfocused type of AD/HD tend to suffer more from obsessive thinking than ritualistic actions. As with other co-occurring conditions, both OCD and AD/HD must be treated.

Post-Traumatic Stress Disorder

The symptoms of post-traumatic stress disorder (PTSD) can occur when an individual perceives an event as a threat to his or her life and safety, or the life and safety of another. Here are a few events that can contribute to the development of PTSD: physical and sexual assaults at any age of development; witnessing violence toward another person; being involved in a plane, train, car, or boating accident; natural disasters; and perceived inability to escape danger. Events that can trigger PTSD in one person may not in another.

Jane Utley Adelizzi, PhD, writes about post-traumatic stress symptoms (PTS). These symptoms and their triggering events do not fall into the diagnostic category of PTSD. Dr. Adelizzi illustrates how children, especially those with AD/HD or learning disabilities, can experience "classroom traumas" that contribute to PTS.[3]

These types of experiences can contribute to some people developing specific symptoms, which include painful recollections and dreams about the event, sleep disturbances, irritability, anger outbursts, difficulty concentrating, and feeling disconnected from others. The other characteristic is avoidance of situations similar to the trauma. If you think you may have PTSD, let your doctor or health-care professional know. Untreated PTSD can make recovery from AD/HD, eating disorders, and addictions difficult if not impossible.

Asberger's Disorder

I knew very little about Asberger's disorder until I started working with a clientele that had an extraordinary amount in common. All were male, were very intelligent, and had AD/HD, and all of them worked in technical aspects of the computer industry. Even more eerie is that most of them were computer programmers. They were financially successful and enjoyed their work—so much that many of them had little or no life outside of it.

Another commonality is that these men lacked social skills. For example, when I met a new client in the waiting room, I introduced myself and extended my hand. Some of these men barely looked at me and didn't notice my extended hand. They shuffled into the office leaving the door open behind them.

This is not to say that anyone who is a computer programmer has Asberger's. Most of these clients were seeking help for their AD/HD symptoms, but some realized they needed help talking and relating with other people. Some clinicians view Asberger's as a syndrome different from autism, where others view it as a milder form of autism. The primary characteristics of Asberger's include a lack of basic social skills such as eye contact and reading facial expressions and body language, as well as balancing talking with listening in conversations. Many who have Asberger's are limited to one or two specific interests, and don't know how to engage with others who are not very similar to themselves. As one man put it, "I only get along with other geeks. Normal people scare me."

The combination of Asberger's disorder and AD/HD can be painful, isolating, and lonely. The lack of ability to form intimate relationships leaves many feeling depressed. Their joy, self-esteem, and social contacts all come from work.

When Asberger's and AD/HD are combined, sufferers need help in the following areas:

- Learning social skills: hand shaking, eye contact, head nodding, smiling
- Practicing social skills in a nonjudgmental setting
- Learning to talk about subjects other than their special interest
- Practicing asking questions of others
- Learning social aspects of interviewing for employment
- Practicing personal hygiene and wearing appropriate attire

Antisocial Personality Disorder

Some of the symptoms of AD/HD can look like antisocial personality disorder (ASPD), which is unfortunate considering those with ASPD are also referred to as "sociopaths" or "psychopaths" and are considered untreatable by most professionals. According to Dwaine McCallon, MD, former prison medical director and expert on both disorders, "ASPD individuals may present symptoms of AD/HD, but this is rare in my experience. The real antisocial personality disorder is very often quite charming, at least superficially, and socially appealing. The common thread in ASPD is the pervasive absence of empathy toward others. The goals in behavior, in planned antisocial acts, and in the pervasive life walk of psychopaths are almost totally self-centered and directed for self-gratification."[4]

Here are some behaviors that are sometimes present in both ASPD and AD/HD:

- Repeatedly performing unlawful acts that are grounds for arrest
- Disregard for, and violation of, the rights of others
- Impulsivity or failure to plan
- Reckless disregard for the safety of self or others
- Consistent irresponsibility, such as inability to hold down a job or honor financial obligations
- Irritability and aggression

There are critical characteristics that differentiate the two disorders, the most important being lack of remorse. People with ASPD show no empathy or regret for their actions, although they may be very sorry they got caught. There are no genuine tears for anyone else they may have hurt. They usually see their victims as the cause for their behavior.

This is very different from those with AD/HD who feel tremendous shame and guilt for their actions. They do not appear righteous or cocky, and they are usually able to take responsibility for their behavior.

Here are some ways to differentiate AD/HD from ASPD:

- Antisocials are often very bright and will guide the evaluator to diagnose them with something other than ASPD.
- Antisocials are usually organized, articulate, and have knowledge of the most recent medications they desire.

- Those with AD/HD often appear scattered, disorganized, and don't hand the evaluator the AD/HD diagnosis.
- Those with AD/HD feel remorse and express empathy without being manipulative.
- People with AD/HD usually do not con others, lie repeatedly, or use an alias.

There are over two million Americans behind bars. A very small percentage of these individuals are dangerous psychopaths. Others, however, are people with undiagnosed or misdiagnosed AD/HD. Without treatment, many spend their lives revolving in and out of jails, prisons, and institutions.

Recognizing Acquired AD/HD

To make the diagnostic picture even more complicated, some people sustain permanent brain damage as a result of their substance abuse. It has been observed that cocaine and amphetamine addicts in particular can have AD/HD-like symptoms with no history of childhood AD/HD. This "acquired" AD/HD is also seen in people with a frontal lobe head injury that can be caused by trauma at birth or a blow to the head.

Now that you have information on how to go about getting evaluated for AD/HD and co-occurring conditions, the next chapter will help you understand the genetic and neurobiological aspects of AD/HD.

IT'S NOT YOUR FAULT, BUT IT IS YOUR PROBLEM

the
biology
of AD/HD
and
addiction

I WAS WET AND cold after spending the night at 8,000 feet with an outdoor counselor, a therapist, and eight alcoholic/addict teenage boys, when I heard something simple yet profound. It was therapist Jen Murphy telling a sobbing, gang-member wannabe, "It's not your fault, but it is your problem."

It's not your fault that you have AD/HD. You haven't done anything wrong. You didn't choose to have AD/HD, and you've gotten this far in life in spite of it. I'm sure you didn't grow up wanting to be an alcoholic, drug abuser, compulsive overeater, or Internet addict either.

If you've been struggling with AD/HD plus any type of addictive behavior that has wreaked havoc with your life, it's time to stop beating yourself up. Both AD/HD and addiction are rooted in your biology. Because you don't have control over your biology, you cannot "will" away your AD/HD traits, just as you can't make yourself taller or shorter. Neither can you wish away your addiction.

Your AD/HD, substance abuse, or behavioral addictions are your problems. You are the one who experiences the consequences of living a life that is out of control. But you're not the only one experiencing frustration, shame, and pain. All those who love you are suffering too. Think about your spouse, partner, parents, children, family, and friends. It's like throwing a stone in a pond. You may be the sinking stone. But your ripples hit those closest to you and continue to wash over others as they expand across the pond.

I want to simplify and synthesize into this chapter hundreds of pages of scientific articles I've read on molecular genetics, neurotransmitters, and brain function. For some of you this may be more information than you want to know; please feel free to read only what is interesting to you. Others may find this information to be oversimplified. For more detailed information, you may read the articles cited in the notes.

I hope that understanding the genetic and biological aspects of AD/HD and addiction will help you or someone you love get treatment. Understanding the physiological roots of your struggle can help dissipate feelings of guilt and shame that prevent you from seeking treatment. Human beings are the only mammals that can, in some cases, override genetic predispositions. You may come from a family whose alcoholism can be traced back through generations, and therefore you may have a predisposition for alcoholism. Yet if you decide to not drink, you won't become an alcoholic. Even if you are suffering from full-blown alcoholism, you can stop and the disease is arrested. If you drink again, alcoholism will come back as bad or worse than it was before.

WHAT CAUSES AD/HD?

AD/HD is believed to be caused primarily by disruption of neurotransmitters in the brain, and in some cases passed on by genetic transmission. Specific types of brain injuries can sometimes cause symptoms indistinguishable from AD/HD and can be considered causal factors. Exposure to drugs, alcohol, and environmental toxins during pregnancy are also being taken into consideration as possible contributing factors of AD/HD. Continued research will give us more information on causes and treatment of AD/HD. Let's begin by looking at the brain.

THIS IS YOUR BRAIN

Different areas of your brain control or regulate your emotions, attention, activity level, memory, information processing, and ability to move, speak, see, and talk. Here are some examples of just a few areas of the brain, which I have added to and adapted from Dr. Daniel Amen's workbook, *Attention Deficit Disorder*.[1]

Prefrontal Cortex: Sometimes referred to as the "executive center" because it sorts input, focuses attention and conscious thought, makes decisions, controls impulses, and communicates with other areas of the brain.

Limbic System: Aids in regulating appetite, sleep, motivation, and sex drive; promotes emotional bonding and processes smells. This is where emotional memories are believed to be stored.

The Basal Ganglia: Helps regulate activity level, helps integrate feelings and body movement, and is a storehouse of learned behavior and programming from the past.

Cingulate System: Allows shifting of attention, helps your mind move from idea to idea and enables you to see options and think expansively.

The Cerebellum: Associated with physical balance and coordination, it also plays a part in balance in conversation and relationship.

The Amygdala, Nucleus Accumbens, and Ventral Tegmental Area (VTA): Among other functions are believed to be key elements in the *reward pathway*.

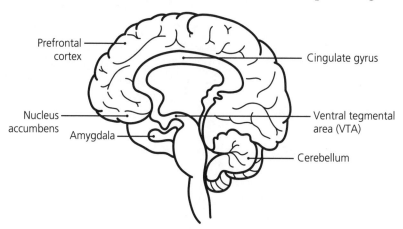

Prefrontal cortex — Cingulate gyrus — Nucleus accumbens — Amygdala — Ventral tegmental area (VTA) — Cerebellum

BRAIN MESSENGERS

Your brain has more than fifty billion intricate cells called neurons. Messages are carried from one neuron to another by chemicals called neurotransmitters. Each neuron depends on thousands of other neurons to carry messages about how you feel and what functions you perform. Sometimes people have too much, too little, or an imbalance in neurotransmitters.

This may create physical and emotional problems, such as the inability to regulate attention and difficulty controlling impulses, and challenges with eating, sleeping, mood, and energy level. These problems can lead to compulsive behaviors, addictions, depression, eating disorders, violent behavior, obsessive-compulsive disorders, and AD/HD, all of which can result in suicide, homicide, domestic violence, child abuse, lost opportunities, and incarcerations.

This is not to say that all these behaviors are purely a result of neurotransmitter imbalance. Other factors play a role, such as the family you grew up in, how you learned to cope with life, exposure to stress and trauma, your resilience, and your ability to learn from your mistakes.

The neurotransmitter dopamine was initially identified as having a role in AD/HD and addiction. Research has expanded the picture to include the role of two others, serotonin and norepinephrine. There are probably more neurotransmitters involved in the AD/HD and addiction picture that will be identified in the future. Let's begin by looking at dopamine.

Dopamine

Dopamine activates and motivates, improves focus and concentration, and gives you a sense of well-being. It is believed that people with AD/HD, impulsive and addictive behaviors, and drug abuse have difficulty utilizing dopamine. Dopamine is also believed to activate the pleasure or reward center of the brain.[2] Most AD/HD medications work by activating dopamine in the brain.

Researchers have located dopamine receptor sites, or places on the neuron that receive dopamine. They have also located defects on genes that determine how the dopamine receptor sites operate. For example, you may have inherited a genetic defect that tells the dopamine receptors to reabsorb the dopamine in the synaptic junction. This means that less dopamine is able to travel the neuron highway to the area of the brain where it is needed.

Serotonin

Variations in the brain's ability to utilize serotonin are linked to depression, low sex drive, sleep disturbances, eating disorders, increased awareness of pain, aggression, obsessive thoughts and compulsive actions, and violent behavior. Many antidepressants such as Prozac, Paxil, Zoloft, and Lexapro are referred to as SSRIs (Selective Serotonin Reuptake Inhibitors) because they stop the reabsorption of serotonin by the neurons that release it, thus increasing serotonin levels and rebalancing the brain's chemistry.

Adequate levels of serotonin help alleviate depression, improve sleep, energy level, and mood, and help decrease behaviors such as binge eating and bulimia.

Recent research has indicated that serotonin may play a part in addiction, though previously the main culprit was thought to be dopamine. One study looked at college students who met the criterion for "binge drinkers," that is, drinking five or more drinks for men, and four or more for women in one sitting. Researchers found that those with a difference on a specific serotonin transporter gene binged on alcohol, drank to get drunk, and drank more alcohol per instance than their peers who did not have the genetic difference.[3]

Researchers have also linked low levels of serotonin to aggression, violence, and suicides.[4] Other research suggests that serotonin levels are lower in people who are impulsive, commit impulsive homicides, and have severe early-onset alcoholism and bulimia.[5]

Decreased serotonin levels also affect cravings for sugar and carbohydrates. Several researchers have connected serotonin imbalance with overeating, binge eating, and bulimia. This may be why SSRI medications are helpful in treating binge eating and bulimia. This also gives us some understanding as to why some people with AD/HD experience relief from symptoms such as impulsiveness, sleep disturbances, agitation, and irritability when prescribed medications that rebalance their serotonin.

Norepinephrine

Norepinephrine has been referred to as the "focus neurotransmitter" and is believed to play a part in memory, learning, attention focusing, and alertness. Like all neurotransmitters, too much or too little norepinephrine can cause problems. Decreased levels of norepinephrine can contribute to a person being easily distracted, depressed, impulsive, and fatigued, and having problems with memory retention and recall. Too much norepinephrine can contribute to high anxiety, aggression, panic states, and violence.

Children with AD/HD were initially treated with stimulant

medication that works on the dopamine system and antide-pressant medications that work with the norepinephrine system. Today there are effective medications that work with norepineph-rine, such as Strattera, or with both dopamine and norepineph-rine, such as Wellbutrin. Research on the roles of neurotransmit-ters will continue to provide us with new medication technology.

THE POWER OF GENETICS

Researchers are able to isolate specific areas of our genes and can associate differences in the coding of certain genes to Down's Syndrome, Sickle Cell Anemia, certain forms of cancer, and vul-nerability to addictions. There has been an explosion of genetic research that identifies genes that may be associated with AD/HD, and that suggest links between AD/HD, addiction, and other disorders. There are five genes identified that impact the trans-portation and reception of dopamine in the brain.[6]

Genetic research has moved beyond the previously held belief that a gene was either dominant or recessive. Researchers are learning that genetic inheritance is extremely complex. You don't just inherit a gene; you also inherit variations in that gene. These variations determine how the gene is expressed. In other words, the same gene can express itself more intensely in the characteristics in one person than it does in another.

Your genes and how they are expressed are passed down to you from previous generations. New understanding of the genetic origin of behaviors and illnesses can help us get beyond moral judgments and shame and move toward solutions. If you're genetically "loaded" for clusters of problems, you can't make that predisposition go away. "Studies in susceptible families suggest that in humans about 50% of the risk for drug addiction is genetic."[7] What you can do is get treatment for your AD/HD and addictions. You can also share with your children and other relatives any genetic predispositions they have. Armed with this information, the next generation will be able to make conscious choices about their involvement with substances and addictive behavior, and they'll be able to choose treatment.

THE BIOLOGY OF ADDICTION

Now that you are familiar with some of the structures of the brain and understand how neurotransmitters work, you are better prepared to learn about the biology of addiction. For years, scientists have identified a reward center in the brain, the area that mediates feelings of pleasure and euphoria, and relief of emotional pain. Your brain needs to distinguish if an experience is pleasurable or not, and tell you if you should repeat or avoid it. It also determines just how rewarding an experience is and creates strong memories about pleasurable experiences, anything from taking drugs to gambling or making love. The more pleasurable the experience, the more your brain will note it and remember it for years to come. This is part of why addicts and alcoholics can have "euphoric recall"—they only remember the pleasure of being drunk, high, or loaded, and forget the pain and misery involved. Dopamine is one of the neurotransmitters involved in the reward center.

Researchers have come to a greater understanding of the effects of dopamine on the reward center through their investigation of "reward deficiency syndrome," which occurs when there is an imbalance of dopamine.[8] When dopamine levels are low, people feel anxious and lose their ability to feel pleasure, setting up cravings for more dopamine. Amazingly, all addictive substances help increase dopamine levels. That's right—from caffeine to nicotine, alcohol to heroin.[9] Foods high in sugar and refined carbohydrates are also believed to increase the release of dopamine in the reward center.

Changes in the Reward Center

Recent research suggests that chronic drug use changes the structure and functions of the brain. Repeated exposure to dopamine-enhancing drugs can contribute to long-lasting adaptations in brain chemistry and the structure of the reward center. Chronic drug use may also alter how individual neurons communicate and interact with each other in the reward center. These changes can last for years after the person stops drug use.[10] This may account for why people who have been abstinent for long periods of time can experience cravings when exposed to movies, graphic pictures, or situations where drugs are being used.

This is an oversimplification, but with addiction, the genetic make-up of some people contributes to their inability to experience natural rewards. They find that alcohol, drugs, certain foods, and high-risk behavior (all believed to increase dopamine) help them feel calm, feel pleasure, or stay focused. A strong memory of the "good" feeling is registered and craving is created. In time it takes more of the substance to create the desired effect. Then tolerance is created. The cravings for dopamine-enhancing substances override the rational, logical part of the brain. People wouldn't risk losing their career, family, and life to eat pickles, because eating pickles doesn't enhance pleasurable and rewarding dopamine.

Why Doesn't Everyone Become Addicted?

A genetic predisposition is not the only cause of addiction. There are a variety of reasons why one person becomes addicted and another doesn't. Some important contributing factors are environment, stress, trauma, life circumstances, and coexisting conditions such as depression, anxiety, post-traumatic stress disorder, and AD/HD.[11] One study notes a sharp increase in the use of substances as adolescents transition into adulthood, and this increase in substance abuse was associated with AD/HD and not any other conditions.[12]

We Repeat What We Learn

If you grew up in a family where drugs, alcohol, or food were used to soothe, numb, or forget problems, you learned this way of handling life's challenges. Alcohol and drug use may have been such an important part of your family life that you assumed all families were like yours. You accepted crazy, addictive, or dysfunctional behavior as normal. This process of normalizing the abnormal contributes to the repetition of substance and behavioral addictions from one generation to the next.

As you understand that a big part of your addiction is rooted in your genetics and brain chemistry, you may feel less shame. Stigma and shame are two factors that may be contributing to your fear and reluctance to get help. The addictions that you have are not your fault, but they are your problem. I hope this chapter has helped you to better understand your situation. In the next chapter we'll look in more detail at the ways we try to self-medicate AD/HD.

FANNING THE FLAMES OF ADDICTION

self-medicating
AD/HD
with
drugs
and
alcohol

THERE IS A BURNING pain inside you. It hurts so badly, all you can think of is putting it out. Drown it, smother it; you'll do anything to stop the burning. And yet, what you use to douse the flames, the substance you choose to throw on the intolerable fire, is gasoline. You pour it on the flames and they rage out of control and finally culminate in an explosion. Too late, you discover you've made the wrong choice. You can kill yourself in your attempts to save yourself. This is what can happen when self-medicating goes wrong.

As human beings we find very creative ways to avoid or alleviate our pain. Whether we suffer from physical, emotional, or spiritual pain, our natural response is to avoid it or stop it. When we self-medicate, we are trying to avoid suffering or trying to feel pleasure.

SELF-MEDICATION

You self-medicate when you use substances, including food or behaviors, to change how you feel: to numb painful feelings, to function better, or to feel intoxicated.

Let's say your doctor prescribes Vicodin after foot surgery. Not only does the Vicodin relieve your physical pain, it makes you feel good. If you keep taking Vicodin when your foot no longer hurts, you are self-medicating. You are taking the Vicodin because it makes you feel good or because it numbs bad feelings.

You may self-medicate because you believe you function better when you're under the influence of substances. For example, you might use cocaine to have the energy to complete a task. You might smoke pot, feeling it enhances your ability to write a song, play computer games, or get through a day of tedious or boring work.

Intoxication is another reason you might self-medicate. Using alcohol and drugs makes you feel good. Euphoric feelings can obliterate emotional pain. Many alcoholics and addicts chase those initial euphoric feelings for years, never quite able to attain them again.

By abusing substances and behaviors, people self-medicate depression, low self-esteem, anxiety, bipolar disorder, obsessive-compulsive disorder, trauma from the past, and AD/HD. Unfortunately, self-medicating is like trying to put out fires with gasoline.

There are two ways people self-medicate. One is with substances: alcohol, marijuana, cocaine, tranquilizers, amphetamines, food, narcotics, nicotine, and caffeine. The other is with compulsive behaviors: gambling, spending, overworking, pornography, and sex or love addictions.

Almost all of us self-medicate at one time or another. You may drink a cup of coffee to stay alert or have a glass of wine after a stressful day. Others find occasional retail therapy (shopping) a way to temporarily feel better. Sometimes you bury yourself in your work until you are ready to deal with situations in your life. Self-medicating on an occasional basis is not terribly destructive, especially if it's a temporary way to deal with a situation or feelings and you soon find other options. However, self-medicating becomes a problem when you use it as a way to avoid or change your feelings and not accept life on its terms.

SELF-MEDICATING AD/HD

I understand the desire to alleviate the pain and humiliation of AD/HD. Living with untreated AD/HD can cause you to feel frustrated, depressed, hopeless, chronically overwhelmed, isolated, ashamed, and full of rage. Abusing substances and having AD/HD can create tremendous feelings of guilt and shame—and eventually, you are self-medicating those too. Not everyone who self-medicates AD/HD will become addicted, but anyone who self-medicates long enough will experience negative consequences.

A staggeringly high number of people with AD/HD are know-ingly or unknowingly self-medicating. Research suggests that as many as 55 percent of adults with AD/HD abuse drugs and alco-hol.[1] If you have AD/HD, you have to be very careful with your use of substances. Even if you don't have a personal or family history of addiction, be cautious. Alcohol and other drugs can make it even harder to manage your AD/HD. If you're one of those who can "take it or leave it," try leaving it. And watch out for how much you do take at those special occasions.

In the rest of this chapter we'll explore how you or someone you love may be using alcohol, illegal and legal drugs, caffeine, or nicotine to treat AD/HD. In the next chapter, we'll discuss self-medicating with food. Let's begin by talking about alcohol.

Alcohol and AD/HD

For people with AD/HD, alcohol can be an attractive solution to their symptoms. Alcohol can calm the physical, emotional, and intellectual restlessness of AD/HD. One woman put it like this: "When I get drunk, my brain disengages, my feelings numb, noises are not as loud. I can be still. My body doesn't have to move. Finally, I get some peace."

But this solution can create even more problems for those with AD/HD. Instead of activating the brain, alcohol "anesthe-tizes" it. This "putting to sleep" impairs concentration, memory function, judgment, and impulse control.

The prefrontal cortex, often referred to as the executive cen-ter of the brain, is like the mission control of a space center. Picture for a moment the many men and women at their com-puters, each playing a vital role in launch, mission, and reentry. Now imagine that one by one, the controllers fall asleep or pass out at their positions. Oops! There go some of the people who control your verbal impulses. As more alcohol reaches the brain, down go the coordination engineers. The folks in the judgment department are snoring. Before you know it, you are on a colli-sion course.

Chronic alcohol abuse can cause long-term or permanent damage to the brain, sometimes resulting in organic brain syn-drome (OBS). Symptoms of OBS range from memory problems to cognitive chaos. Korsakoff syndrome is a type of organic brain syndrome characterized by impairments in acquiring new information or establishing new memories, as well as retrieving previous memories. People with Korsakoff's will confabulate, fabricate, or make up information to fill in memory gaps.

This is another place where AD/HD and substance abuse intersect. Some people with AD/HD who do not abuse substances have chronic and severe memory gaps due to inattention and cognitive problems. Filling in memory gaps becomes a way of life. Add even small amounts of alcohol to the AD/HD brain, and say "good-bye" to your working memory for awhile.

Sometimes those with histories of long-term drug or alcohol abuse don't completely respond to treatment for their AD/HD. Years into recovery, they continue to have severe cognitive impairments. They don't improve much, even with medication. Their brains are so damaged that they cannot completely heal. It's important to sort out OBS and AD/HD in the drug and alcoholic population.

Marijuana and AD/HD

Many longtime pot smokers cling to their beliefs that marijuana is natural, harmless, and not addictive, in spite of research and literature that clearly states otherwise. The effects of marijuana or cannabis on the brain are not thoroughly understood. Research suggests that cannabis works by indirectly increasing dopamine in the reward center of the brain, contributing to its addictive potential.[2] Marijuana can impair neurotransmitter function, diminish concentration, cloud thinking, decrease motivation, disturb sleep cycles, damage motor coordination, alter depth perception, and disrupt hormonal functioning.

Marijuana is a drug of choice for many with AD/HD (especially young people). Pot appears to affect the AD/HD brain differently. Pot smokers with AD/HD not only report feeling calm when stoned, they also report feeling energized, with increased ability to focus their attention. The problem is that if they smoke a bit too much or the marijuana is potent, they end up stoned, immobilized, dazed, and confused. Pot smoking actually makes AD/HD symptoms worse. The feelings of euphoria and relaxation override the abusers' ability to accurately judge how pot smoking is affecting their functioning.

Some with AD/HD are not able to stop smoking long enough to even have a trial on medication. Others will stop or decrease smoking long enough to try medicine, but find they prefer the effects of pot smoking. No matter what pot smokers believe, marijuana is not a drug that treats AD/HD.

Ecstasy and AD/HD

Ecstasy has special appeal to substance abusers with AD/HD, because it has properties of both stimulants and hallucinogens. Like other street drugs, Ecstacy varies in potency and may also include ingredients such as caffeine, ephedra, and crudely made speed.

The drug is frequently taken at "raves," at concerts, and in clubs. Ecstasy can disrupt the body's ability to control temperature, causing severe overheating and dehydration. Symptoms of an ecstasy overdose include profuse sweating, dehydration, exhaustion, dramatic rises in body temperature and blood pressure, seizures, and loss of consciousness, which in severe cases can result in heart failure, stroke, and death. Some ecstasy users have died the first or second time they used the drug. Ecstasy and AD/HD are a bad combination.

Amphetamines and AD/HD

Amphetamines, or "speed," are stimulant drugs. When people take them in high doses, they feel euphoric and energized. To get higher with smaller amounts, some people turn to injecting, snorting, or smoking amphetamines. There are no precise statistics on the percentage of people with AD/HD who abuse amphetamines. However, my clinical observations and those of some of my colleagues suggest that amphetamines and cocaine are drugs of choice for many with AD/HD. They accidentally found a street drug that helped their AD/HD symptoms. Some of these people were able to put the drug down when their "solution" turned into a new and ravenous problem; others could not and became addicted.

I have worked with people who have used a prescribed amphetamine to lose weight. Often I hear that while the appetite suppressant did not suppress their appetite, they sure got a lot done. Some people look back fondly on the time they were prescribed an amphetamine. One woman said, "I didn't lose weight, but I was able to think clearly, focus on what was in front of me, and finish what I started. The weird thing is that I felt calm. I wasn't blowing up at my family. My life became more manageable. My doctor took me off them because they weren't helping me lose weight. But I haven't felt right since." The amphetamines were working, not for her obesity, but for her undiagnosed AD/HD.

Amphetamines have been prescribed over the years to treat AD/HD. The amount of amphetamine or stimulant medication used to treat AD/HD is only a tiny portion compared to what is used on the streets to get high. With street amphetamines, you're never sure of the dosage or the contents of what you take, and you risk the dangers of using needles, overdosing, and incarceration.

When properly and closely monitored by a professional with expertise in AD/HD and addictions, amphetamine treatment for AD/HD can be highly effective. We will talk more about pre-scribed medication to treat AD/HD in those who have histories of addiction in chapter 14.

Cocaine and AD/HD

Cocaine has a similar appeal for the person with AD/HD as amphetamines, even though there are differences. Cocaine provides a greater sense of euphoria and well-being. However, the effects of cocaine do not last as long as the effects of amphetamines; therefore, the user must use cocaine more frequently to maintain the desired effect. Cocaine addicts can quickly find themselves in trouble trying to pay for a habit that no longer feels good. The desire for cocaine can be so powerful that they will give anything, including their lives, for it.

Initially, cocaine was believed to be only psychologically addicting. However, over the years professionals have witnessed the physically and emotionally addictive properties of the drug. This is especially true of "crack" cocaine, where the drug is pre-pared so that it can be smoked. Smoking cocaine gets more of the drug into the bloodstream immediately.

Many people with AD/HD who have had experience with cocaine report that it initially felt like a wonder drug. It not only helped them concentrate better, it made them feel calm and dissipated their feelings of shame and self-hatred. Before they realized it, they were experiencing serious cocaine-related problems.

Narcotics and AD/HD

Heroin is often the drug that comes to mind when thinking about narcotics. Most of us have images of heroin addicts, but what about your neighbor, child's teacher, or accountant who is addicted to Talwin, Vicodin, Percocet, codeine, or OxyContin? Abuse and addiction to prescription narcotics are on the rise. It has become easy to obtain narcotics over the Internet without a prescription. Some manufacturers are reputable while others are not. You may be buying the pharmaceutical equivalent of the drug you order, or you may be purchasing drugs that are laced with other drugs and contain bacteria or toxins used in the manufacturing process.

For people with AD/HD, narcotic drugs provide a calming and sometimes stimulating effect that some say no other drug could ever match. Narcotics can decrease AD/HD restlessness of the body and brain. They can also turn irritable, agitated, aggressive people into passive, "nodding out," loaded people who couldn't care less about what's going on around them. This "high," which is actually a low, can be very inviting for the person with AD/HD. If you have ever been under the influence of narcotics intentionally, or have used them to treat pain after surgery or dental work, you may remember being quite docile, feeling like everything was okay, and not really caring about anything. Or you may remember feeling energized and very happy while washing your windows and cleaning out your closet.

Heroin addiction is becoming more prevalent among children and adolescents who smoke the drug. Many adolescents feel immortal and immune to the dangers of using heroin. Very few practicing heroin addicts die of old age. Heroin overdose is just one reason for this. One of the problems of self-medicating with street drugs is that you never know how pure and potent the drug you are using really is. The person with AD/HD may be more apt to test the limits of what his or her body can tolerate. As a result, AD/HD narcotic abusers and addicts are more likely than others to die from an overdose by combining street or prescription narcotics with cocaine and alcohol.

Caffeine and AD/HD

Oh, the joys of that morning cup of coffee or tea. Caffeine is caffeine, whether we get it from chocolate, cola, iced tea, or a double espresso. Research has bounced back and forth for decades trying to prove the hazards of caffeine, especially in the form of coffee. The controversy rages, and meanwhile Americans continue to consume coffee, tea, and caffeinated sodas.

People with AD/HD frequently activate their frontal lobes with caffeine. I have a friend who was drinking thirty-six cups of coffee a day. Now that his AD/HD is being treated with medication, his caffeine use has plummeted. Caffeine consumption is a frequent topic with my clients. They often struggle with cutting down their daily caffeine intake. This is especially true if they are on stimulant medication to treat their AD/HD. Caffeine can react with the medication, resulting in anxiety, tremors, and agitation.

I remember one man I worked with who was proud of never using caffeine to self-medicate his AD/HD. About a year into treatment he had an "ah ha" insight when he shared with me that he hadn't taken any NoDoz (which is pill-form caffeine) since he'd been on medication. "You know, I used to buy a box of NoDoz whenever I had a project to complete. I would chew up the box of tablets and work for hours. It was amazing how I could finish my project." This man was able to laugh at his denial about ever using caffeine to enhance his ability to stay alert and complete projects.

His experience is not unique. Some people with AD/HD use over-the-counter diet pills and appetite suppressants; others abuse cold medications that contain ephedrine, which can have a stimulating effect on some people. (Ephedrine has been taken off the market due to its lethal side effects, such as heart attacks.)

While self-medicating with caffeine may not be as dangerous as other drugs, ultimately it's not an effective choice for treating AD/HD. Too much caffeine can result in stomach irritation, anxiety, increased blood pressure, tremors, and agitation. If you are taking medication, be especially careful about your caffeine intake because it can cause a synergistic reaction with the medication. This doesn't mean that it increases the effects of your medication, rather it increases the negative effects of caffeine. It's best to decrease your caffeine intake as you begin taking medication. Many find that when their medication is stabilized they no longer crave caffeine.

Nicotine and AD/HD

Nicotine is a readily available, insidious, and powerfully addictive drug that, like few other drugs, has both stimulating and relaxing effects. It is second only to food in the series of drugs children use to self-medicate their AD/HD. Many people kick addictions to opiates, cocaine, alcohol, pot, and prescription medications, yet are not able to quit smoking.

Nicotine is incredibly seductive, especially to people with AD/HD. Immediately after the first inhalation, nicotine sets off a chain reaction that ultimately causes a release of dopamine in the brain, affecting pleasure, motivation, and concentration. Smokers often report an increase in alertness and focus immediately after smoking. They also report feeling calm and relaxed. Because nicotine is quickly broken down by enzymes in the body, the effects of nicotine are short-lived. The smoker goes into withdrawals and needs to light up again.

Even people without AD/HD express frustration about their inability to stop smoking, but it seems to be especially difficult for those with AD/HD. Their impulsiveness, compulsiveness, and need to stimulate and calm their brains make it even harder to quit and maintain their abstinence.

There are options today that weren't available ten years ago. Nicotine patches, gum, inhalants, and nose spray can help smokers wean themselves off the drug. (But beware: nicotine products can be addicting if not used as directed.)

As mentioned throughout this book, medications that were initially designed to treat one condition are sometimes found to be useful in treating another condition. This is true of bupropion (Wellbutrin). People who were taking bupropion for depression found that they had less desire to smoke. That makes perfect sense, because bupropion primarily works by activating dopamine and norepinephrine. It works so well that the manufacture took 50 mg of bupropion and marketed it under the name of Zyban, to help those kicking the smoking habit. Because Wellbutrin works with the neurotransmitters dopamine and norepinephrine, it is also used to treat AD/HD.

Prescription Drugs and AD/HD

Well-meaning physicians can contribute to prescription drug abuse and addiction by not adequately assessing their patients' condition. Sometimes, people will feign illness or injuries to get the prescription medications they abuse. They may be taking painkillers to deaden feelings rather than physical pain. They may be using tranquilizers and sleeping pills to slow down their bodies and brains. Self-medicating with prescribed medications can lead to addictions and all the consequences that come with being an addict.

You or someone you know may be operating as a kind of lay pharmacist, creatively combining drugs to help yourself feel better, to numb your pain, or to enhance your functioning. This is especially true of people with untreated AD/HD.

Most people use prescribed medication appropriately. They are clear as to why they are taking the medication. When the condition they are being treated for goes away, they stop taking the medication and have no craving for more. They may throw out the unused portion of a codeine or Vicodin or Valium prescription. This would be unthinkable for an addict.

Trying to self-medicate AD/HD is, at best, inefficient, and at worst, dangerous or fatal. Now that you understand the process of self-medicating, ask yourself who is in the best position to medicate your AD/HD: you or your doctor?

ACCEPTANCE — THE BEGINNING OF RECOVERY

It is impossible to get help if you don't think you have a problem. For many, their denial is their biggest problem. People in your life may be telling you that you have an alcohol, drug, spending, eating, or Internet problem. They may also be telling you that your forgetfulness, impulsive actions, and inability to stay focused for more than a millisecond are painful to be around. If you've read this far, you may be aware that something in your life isn't working.

It's easy to accept good things; it's much harder to accept tragedy, missed opportunities, and illness. Acceptance of our difficulties is a process. We don't just automatically accept the death of a loved one, the diagnosis of AD/HD, or our addictions. The process of acceptance usually begins with denial, and then anger. We progress through bargaining, depression, and finally, acceptance. Notice that acceptance is at the end of the process. It's common to bounce in and out of these stages and not experience them in sequence. If you do not interrupt this process by self-medicating, and get help when you need it, you will eventually move through all of the stages.

You don't have to like what happens to you in your life, but the ability to accept what you cannot change is essential. Acceptance is liberating. It can provide you with the freedom to get the help you need and the treatment you deserve.

We'll talk about that help at length in chapters 13, 14, and 15, but first let's explore some other ways we self-medicate with behaviors.

WHEN FOOD CAN'T FIX IT

overindulging
and
eating
disorders

DO YOU EVER HIDE your ice cream in the back of the freezer under frozen vegetables and ice trays? Maybe you keep stashes of food hidden in your home, garage, or office, so others won't eat it. Are you obsessed with eating, not eating, dieting, or body image? Do you feel that you are not in control of your eating?

If you relate to some of the above questions, you may be using food to self-medicate your AD/HD symptoms. Having problems with food doesn't mean you have AD/HD. This chapter will help you clearly identify your problems with food, and may help you identify and understand a loved one's eating problems. You'll also learn ways to change your eating and AD/HD behavior.

Not everyone with AD/HD will overindulge in food or develop eating disorders. Similar to drug and alcohol addiction, there are many factors that contribute to problems with food—genetics, biology, environment, and learned behavior. Participating in activities that require thinness, such as modeling, dancing, and gymnastics, also contributes to eating disorders.

It is especially important to be aware of the signs of eating disorders in adolescents with and without AD/HD. Most eating disorders develop during childhood, adolescence, and young adulthood. Eating disorders don't only affect females; they are on the rise among boys and men. Those with AD/HD may be at greater risk of developing an eating disorder. Eating disorders can be lethal. Early intervention and treatment increase the chances of recovery.

Although we don't think of food as a drug, it can be used as one. We have to eat to live, but eating too much or too little of certain types of food can be harmful. Because there is no way to abstain from eating, food addictions and eating disorders are extremely hard to recover from. An addict would find it impossible to have one drink, one cigarette, or one line of coke three times a day, and no more. Yet this is what those with eating disorders are faced with. Not only do they have to eat, many prepare meals for their families. They may have to abstain from certain foods, perhaps those containing sugar or refined carbohydrates, because these foods trigger a compulsion for more. Yet everywhere they look they see these foods.

Food is not only legal and necessary, it's often the centerpiece of social events. Eating is a culturally acceptable way of comforting ourselves, yet paradoxically, our culture is obsessed with thinness. "Food is good, but don't gain weight." No wonder so many become imprisoned in binge-purge cycles, chronic dieting, and anorexia nervosa.

We'll discuss different eating disorders in detail and look at the role of neurotransmitters. But before we do that, take a few minutes, if you like, to answer some questions about your relationship with food.

Please check all boxes that are *yes* answers:

☐ Do you wake up each morning thinking about what you will or won't eat that day?

☐ Do you eat more than you intend to?

☐ Do you find yourself unaware of how much you have eaten?

☐ Are there times when you can't stop eating until you feel sick?

☐ Do you crave foods that are high in sugar and carbohydrates (pasta, cookies, bread, potatoes)?

☐ Do you have cravings for salty foods such as potato chips, French fries, or pretzels?

☐ Do you eat to soothe your anger, sadness, loneliness, depression, or boredom?

☐ Do you use caffeine or sugar throughout the day to keep your energy level up?

☐ Are you frequently trying new diets or using weight-loss products?

☐ Do you binge (eat large amounts of food in a short period of time)?

☐ Do certain foods trigger a binge?

☐ Have you ever caused yourself to vomit after eating?

☐ Do you feel euphoric or calm after you purge?

☐ Do you deny yourself food when you are hungry?

☐ Do you see yourself as fat, even though people tell you that you are thin?

☐ Do you take over-the-counter appetite suppressants?

☐ Have you ever taken prescribed medication to help you lose weight?

☐ Have you used laxatives or enemas to lose weight?

☐ Has a health care professional told you that your weight is unhealthy?

☐ Have you had medical problems as a result of your eating?

☐ Does eating while doing tasks improve your concentration?

☐ Are you ashamed or do you feel guilty about your eating?

Now take a moment to reflect on the questions to which you answered yes. You don't need to count the number of yes answers.

Look at the specific issues you may have identified. Be gentle with yourself and appreciate your willingness to take a hard look at your eating. It takes courage to do what you just did.

HOW AD/HD CONTRIBUTES TO EATING PROBLEMS

There is little research on AD/HD and eating disorders. However, one study on obesity concluded that over 30 percent of seriously overweight adults had symptoms of AD/HD that contributed to their difficulty in changing their eating pattern.[1] In another study, subjects exhibited a decreased ability to recognize internal signals such as hunger, thirst, or being full. The bottom line is, "half of the subjects in this study were unaware of, or inattentive to, many of the physical and psychological factors that can modify eating behavior and hence weight control."[2]

Eating disorders such as binge eating, bulimia, compulsive overeating, and anorexia are all characterized by loss of control, which, as we know, is a primary characteristic of AD/HD. You may not have control over what and how much you eat. Your AD/HD brain may be hijacked by your cravings for foods you know are not good for you and later regret eating.

Similar to drug and alcohol abuse, food can be used to medicate the pain of many problems and disorders, including AD/HD. Food can calm your physical and emotional restlessness, or stimulate your mind to stay alert and attentive. You may be trying to eat your way out of feeling inadequate and incompetent.

Difficulties with organization can make it harder for you to shop for food and prepare meals. I remember a marketing executive with AD/HD whose goal was to prepare a dinner of a baked potato, chicken, and a salad. After five months of AD/HD treatment that included medication, she accomplished her goal. Many with AD/HD are "cooking-challenged." The shame and pain they experience (especially women) can become grounds for self-medicating.

Back to Those Neurotransmitters

If you've read the previous few chapters, you're familiar with the role neurotransmitters play in AD/HD and addiction. The same neurotransmitters—serotonin and dopamine—play a role in overindulging and eating disorders. Sugars and carbohydrates such as cookies, bread, and pasta temporarily increase serotonin in your brain. Foods high in sugar can temporarily increase dopamine in your brain's reward center.

When Enough Is Enough

One of the functions of serotonin is to tell the brain when you are satiated and have had enough to eat. If your brain is not utilizing serotonin properly, it can be hard to know when you are full.[3] Low levels of serotonin are also believed to contribute to depression, sleep problems, and impulsive behavior. This is why medications that increase serotonin utilization are often used to treat binge eating and bulimia.

Dopamine

Recent research is also linking dopamine as a player in the realm of problematic eating. Several studies are looking at how sugar affects the reward pathways in the brain by activating the release of dopamine. Other studies are looking at the relationship between dopamine and obesity. "It's possible that obese people have fewer dopamine receptors because their brains are trying to compensate for having chronically high dopamine levels, which are triggered by chronic overeating," says researcher Gene-Jack Wang. "However, it's also possible that these people have low numbers of dopamine receptors to begin with, making them more vulnerable to addictive behaviors including compulsive food intake."[4]

For the purpose of examining the ways people self-medicate AD/HD with food, we'll divide this problem into several areas: undereating, compulsive overeating, binge eating, bulimia, anorexia, and addiction to sugar. First, let's talk about an eating problem that affects some people with AD/HD.

Undereating

Some people with AD/HD become hyperfocused and forget to eat. Their attention is so captivated or distracted that they are not aware of their hunger until it's overwhelming. Then they're ravenous and grab the first thing they find, often fast or junk foods.

Some thin people with AD/HD may be misdiagnosed as having anorexia. In the same way that we should not diagnose AD/HD solely by hyperactivity, anorexia cannot be diagnosed by thinness alone. There are complex cognitive and behavior patterns that are important to explore to make an accurate diagnosis. Those whose low body weight is not caused by anorexia often learn to eat more regularly and more nutritiously when their AD/HD is treated. They can even gain weight when taking stimulant medication, which enables them to be aware of feeling hungry, stop what they are doing, and eat. Education and medication can also help those with AD/HD to have healthy food on hand and to organize meals.

Compulsive Overeating

People overeat at times. You may eat because the food is delicious, even if you're not hungry, or you may eat more than you intend at a potluck or Thanksgiving dinner. But for some, overeating becomes a compulsion they can't control. Compulsive overeaters use food to alter their feelings rather than to satisfy hunger. They may eat because they feel anxious, stressed, angry, or bored. They tend to crave foods high in carbohydrates, sugars, and salt, which can alter their neurotransmitter levels. For some compulsive overeaters, once they start eating, the feelings (or numbing of feelings) are so powerful they can't stop.

Eating can temporarily calm AD/HD physical and mental restlessness. Eating can ground some people with AD/HD, helping them focus better while reading, studying, or watching television. If your brain is not quick to contain your impulses, you will eat without thinking. Some compulsive overeaters are shocked to realize they have finished a carton of ice cream or a family-size bag of M&M's. They weren't consciously aware of how much they were eating. It's as though they had gone into a trance.

Binge Eating

Binge eating differs from compulsive overeating. Buying the food and finding the time and place to binge in secret can create a level of risk and excitement that the AD/HD brain craves. The binge itself may only last fifteen to twenty minutes. It usually includes foods high in sugars and highly refined carbohydrates, which have immediate and very gratifying properties.

The binge eater is compelled to eat as much as possible, desperately attempting to relieve anxiety and feel calm. Similar to addicts, once the binge eater begins bingeing, logical thoughts about how they will feel later vanish.

The relief is short-lived, and soon feelings of shame, guilt, and miserable fullness take over. Some people can only stand the aftermath of bingeing for so long before they start purging.

Bulimia

Bulimia is binge eating accompanied by purging. Purging is the process of eliminating food by self-induced vomiting and/or using laxatives or enemas. Shortly after feeling calmed and exhausted by the satiation the binge provided, the bulimic becomes obsessed with removing the food and calories. The bulimic now seeks relief by purging. Many bulimics report entering an altered state of consciousness, experiencing feelings of calmness and euphoria after they vomit. But as soon as anxieties resurface, the bulimic is bingeing again.

Untreated AD/HD can contribute to the vicious cycle of bulimia. Because bulimics perform their rituals in secret, they tend to become more and more isolated. The shame and isolation can be compounded by shame of their AD/HD behaviors. Some people with eating disorders are not able to recover until their AD/HD is treated.

Liz has been uncomfortable with her body since she was a child. Her family teased her mercilessly because she was "chubby." Liz found that eating candy when studying during college helped her concentrate. She later found that bingeing and purging helped her survive a very abusive relationship until she was able to get out. Sometimes she would binge and purge four to six times a day.

Once out of the relationship, Liz was able to get treatment for her bulimia. Even though she was constantly obsessed with thoughts of food and her body image, Liz was able to contain her bingeing for years. But like many bulimics, life changes and stress triggered the dormant obsession to binge, and the out of control binge-purge cycle returned with a vengeance.

Today Liz is making progress with her bulimia. She still binges occasionally, but rarely purges. The diagnosis and treatment of her AD/HD has helped her to become aware of the feeling that precedes a binge and aided in her ability to control her impulses. Liz is a very attractive woman. From the outside no one would ever guess that she suffers from an eating disorder. Bulimia can be a hidden disorder for those who are not extremely thin or overweight. Most people have no idea how many waking hours the bulimic spends obsessing on food. The same is true for the anorectic.

Anorexia

Many professionals view anorexia as a disorder of control. If you are ever in conversation with someone who has anorexia, you'll feel their despair and loss of control. No one wants to measure the same potato three times because it looks larger than three ounces, but that's the life of someone with anorexia. Anorexia nervosa can be deadly.

Anorectics have lost control of their ability to eat or to monitor their eating in a healthy way. They are obsessed with thoughts of food, body image, and diet. Most doctors, psychiatrists, and therapists see anorexia as being rooted in the family one grew up in, enmeshment with a parent, perfectionism, and a high need for control. Paradoxically, this all leads to a profound loss of control. Anorectics can't control their repetitive thoughts about food, calories, and body image. They may use laxatives, diuretics, enemas, and compulsive exercise to maintain their distorted body image. Anorectics whose skeletal anatomy is visible can still see their emaciated bodies as having too much fat in certain places.

As we learn more about AD/HD, we discover that people manifest AD/HD traits differently. Some with AD/HD get stuck on thoughts and behaviors, have trouble seeing other options, and become preoccupied with details. They can't stop listening to their inner critic who says things to them that are so harsh, mean, and cruel that they would never think of saying such horrible things to anyone else. Obsessing on food, exercise, and thinness gives the anorectic a way to focus his or her chaotic AD/HD brain.

Another reason anorectic behaviors are attractive to some people with AD/HD is that it is hard to be hyperactive when your body is starving. Frequently, these people will only become aware of their high level of activity, distractibility, or impulsiveness after they have been in recovery from anorexia.

Being distracted and spaced-out are characteristics of both anorexia and bulimia, whether or not they are accompanied by AD/HD. In each case the ability to concentrate is hampered by insufficient nourishment of the brain. For people with AD/HD, however, there is a history of attention difficulties that predates the eating disorder. Their concentration, impulse problems, and activity level may not improve when their eating disorder is treated. As a matter of fact, their AD/HD traits can get worse once they are no longer self-medicating with food or organizing their lives around food and exercise. If you have struggled with eating disorders and you suspect you may have AD/HD, it's important to get an evaluation. Both your eating disorder and your AD/HD must be treated.

Addiction to Sugar

Most people enjoy eating foods containing sugar, and do not develop intense cravings or addiction to it. Why is it that some people become obsessed and addicted to sugar? Some of the answers go back to the neurotransmitter level. We discussed earlier that people with AD/HD may have decreased levels of dopamine and so unwittingly find ways to get that dopamine up. Studies with rats suggest that sugar increases dopamine levels that provide feelings of pleasure.[5] Another study suggests that rats had symptoms of withdrawal similar to those of heroin addicts when a high level of sugar intake was abruptly stopped.[6]

Some adults with AD/HD readily admit that they are addicted to sugar, especially chocolate, which also contains caffeine. They find that eating sugar helps them stay alert, calm, and focused. Prior to AD/HD treatment, some report drinking a six pack of sugary soda, drinking several cups of coffee with sugar, and nibbling on candy and sweets throughout the day.

Are you someone who craves, overindulges, or shows signs of addiction to chocolate? You may know someone who calls themselves a chocoholic. Why do people with and without AD/HD crave chocolate? Because it makes them feel good. Besides the sugar and caffeine, chocolate contains tryptophan, a precursor to serotonin. Another chemical in chocolate is phenylethylamine (the "love chemical"), which is believed to release dopamine in the reward center of your brain. Chocolate fulfills several of the neurotransmitter needs that the person with AD/HD may crave.

TREATMENT FOR AD/HD AND EATING DISORDERS

Both AD/HD and eating disorders must be aggressively treated. It can be difficult, if not impossible, to stabilize your eating without treating your AD/HD. On the other hand, you may be getting treatment for your AD/HD, yet suffering from life-threatening eating disorders. It is tricky to stabilize binge eating, bulimia, and anorexia, while also treating AD/HD. The important thing is to find professionals with experience in treating AD/HD and eating disorders, and to make sure you are being treated comprehensively. You may have to educate your healthcare professional on your coexisting conditions. You may also have to work with more than one professional, one to treat your AD/HD and another to treat your eating disorders. Recovering takes time.

Be patient with yourself as you journey toward a healthier life. A comprehensive treatment program includes:

- An eating disorder assessment by an eating disorder specialist
- Evaluation for and treatment of AD/HD
- A complete physical examination
- Work with a nutritionist if possible
- Exercise programs (that are monitored if you are a compulsive exerciser)
- Participation in groups such as Overeaters Anonymous, Weight Watchers
- Therapy and support groups for eating disorders
- Medication when warranted to treat AD/HD, eating disorders, and other coexisting conditions
- Identifying trigger foods and abstaining from them
- Therapy or coaching that helps you adapt to your AD/HD

Medication

You may need medication to treat your AD/HD and eating disorder at the neurotransmitter level. Even if you feel embarrassed talking about your eating problems, don't let it keep you from getting help. Explain to your doctor how your AD/HD affects your daily life. Tell him or her the details of your eating problems. It's the only way you can get the help you need.

If you have abused prescription or street amphetamines or over-the-counter appetite suppressants, you may not be a good candidate for amphetamine-based medication such as Adderall and Dexadrine. (Ritalin and Concerta are not amphetamines.) This doesn't mean you absolutely can't take amphetamines to treat your AD/HD. Be honest with your doctor about your history of amphetamine abuse. You and your doctor make the decision about stimulant medication, and the decision depends on your history of abuse and where you are in your addiction recovery. The few people I know who have developed a tolerance to and abused stimulant medication have histories of abusing prescribed and street amphetamines. There are nonstimulant medications such as Wellbutrin and Strattera that treat AD/HD.

Keep Yourself Stimulated

Many people with AD/HD need high levels of novelty and stimulus in their daily lives. Take responsibility for living a life that is stimulating. Boredom can trigger eating problems. Don't just be open to new opportunities—create them. You might be more willing to travel, try a new sport, or find a hobby when you accept that being stimulated is an essential part of treating your eating problems.

Exercise

Regular exercise is essential for healthy bodies and minds, and those with AD/HD have a greater need for it. Exercise decreases stress and can exhaust your hyperactive body and restless brain. Exercise is also crucial for those with eating disorders. Aerobic exercise in particular increases all those wonderful neurotransmitters we've been talking about, thus decreasing the need to self-medicate. However, compulsive exercise can accompany eating disorders—so please be aware if your exercising starts becoming compulsive. If you have abused exercise in the past, make sure you have a coach, trainer, or friend who will support you.

Look for fun ways to get exercise. Not everyone enjoys working out on the same machines at the loud overcrowded gym several times a week. Go for walks, hikes, or bike rides with family or friends. Work in your garden or find home improvement projects that interest you. There are organized sports for people of all ages. It's not too late to learn a new sport like tennis, volleyball, or skiing.

Climb On

Rock climbing at the gym or outdoors helps me stay fit. My mind is stimulated by the ever-changing terrain and the challenge of climbing higher and better. Although rock climbing is not a sport for most people, for me, it's a metaphor for living. There are times when I look at a mountain and think, *There is no way I'm going to get up that.* Yet with my harness and helmet, I make the reaches and take the steps as I inch my way toward the top. I frequently get stuck and see no way to keep climbing. If I don't give up, I eventually find a crack to put my fingers or toes in. Sometimes my arms and legs are burning with fatigue. If I fall or have to let go, I have no choice but to trust my harness and the person belaying me as I hang a hundred feet in the air. I've been know to yell, curse, and ask God for help as I search for the smallest nub to place a few fingers or toes on.

Getting to the top is a powerful feeling, but not the goal.

Climbing is about using inner resources that I'm not aware I have. It's about finding creative ways to get to places beyond my reach. Climbing is also about trusting my judgment, my body, my equipment, and the people on the ground who hold my life in their hands. I don't have great technique or style. I don't care about "looking good," I just get up the mountain any way I can. I'm telling you this because I've found it to be so helpful in many areas of my life as well as in the lives of my clients who climb and people I teach to climb. Please don't let AD/HD, eating disorders, or any other addictions keep you from climbing to places you believe are beyond your reach. Trust your inner resources and the people in your life who support you.

In the next chapter, we'll talk about "behavioral addictions"—things people can't seem to stop doing, even when their lives are being destroyed.

WHEN YOU CAN'T STOP DOING IT

self-medicating
with
addictive
behaviors

ABUSING SUBSTANCES ISN'T THE only way we attempt to put out the fires of AD/HD. Some people use behaviors to numb feelings, feel better, or stimulate their brains.

Because many with AD/HD also have difficulties controlling impulses, you can see how easy it might be to become a compulsive spender, gambler, day trader, worker, or sex and love addict. We can become addicted to any behavior, even those that are good for us (in proper balance) such as exercising or working. If you lose your ability to control your behavior in spite of negative consequences, you are addicted.

Do you find yourself engaging in behaviors you know are not good for you? And you can't stop doing them? Do you promise your family you will work less, and then stay late at the office or bring work home? Do you feel like you or a loved one is glued to the chair in front of the computer? It's not the behavior but your inability to control it that causes problems.

Your addictions can occur in real or virtual time. With easy access to the Internet, most behavioral addictions can be played out online, thus creating Internet addictions. Let's start by exploring this relatively new arena of addictive behavior.

INTERNET ADDICTIONS

Using the Internet is not an addiction for most people, yet for some their compulsive use has devastating consequences. It makes sense that people with AD/HD would be attracted to the World Wide Web, because cruising the Internet is similar to how the AD/HD brain works. There is no wrong way to cruise the Internet. How perfect for the AD/HD brain, which tends to over-focus when stimulated.

There are a variety of Internet addictions: shopping, surfing for information, chatting, gambling, "gaming" or playing games with others, pornography, online auctioning, and stock day trading. People can have most of these addictions without the Internet; yet easy accessibility to the Internet has made them more prevalent. With a computer, you don't have to get organized to leave your home to go shopping, auctioning, meet people to chat with, or place a bet. You can use, abuse, or become addicted to activities on the Internet in the comfort of your own home.

Net Compulsions

Net compulsions are a category of Internet addiction that includes compulsive online stock trading, compulsive online gambling, and compulsive online auction addiction. Net compulsions are fueled by the excitement and "rush" of bidding, betting, and winning. The day trader is basically betting on the mood of the market that day. The day trader can spend countless hours overfocusing on his or her investment and trying to buy and sell stocks at the precise time to make a profit. Unfortunately most day traders, especially those with AD/HD, lose.

Some with AD/HD become enthralled with bidding, buying, and selling through online auctions. They optimistically see online auctioning as a way of making a living. Yet most spend an inordinate amount of time to make very little money. Online auctioning is not a great career move for most people with AD/HD.

Online Gaming

A new cultural phenomenon that can be found in epidemic proportions predominately among boys and young adult males is "Gaming" or playing games with others on the Internet. Part of what's so engaging about gaming is that "gamers" not only play against each other, they also chat with friends and create new friendships. The gamer can build a tolerance to gaming and need to spend more hours on the computer to feel good. Gaming becomes problematic when the gamer spends more time playing and relating on the computer than in real time, thus depriving him from developing social skills. Sleep is compromised, grades can plummet, and socializing with friends and family becomes almost non-existent.

Gaming is especially seductive for those with AD/HD. One shy fourteen-year-old said, "Gaming gives me a safe spot where I can be who I really am inside." Parents of AD/HD gamers have reported that their children experience withdrawal symptoms such as depression, agitation, irritability, and crying when Internet privileges are eliminated.

Help for Internet Addictions

- Be aware of how much time you are actually spending on the Internet.
- Ask yourself if the Internet is consuming time you could spend with family and friends or time you could be working or sleeping.
- Set limits on the amount of Internet time kids and teenagers have per day and stick to them. This isn't easy and takes supervision.
- Find out what needs you are self-medicating on the Internet and get help. This may include counseling, making changes in relationships, and finding ways of having fun.
- You may have to abstain from Internet use completely, or you may be able to abstain from the areas to which you are addicted.

Ironically, help for Internet addiction is available on the Internet. See appendix D for websites and books that will provide you with resources.

Now let's look at behaviors we can become addicted to both online and in real time.

GAMBLING

Some people enjoy an occasional trip to Reno or buying lottery tickets once in a while. Their gambling is not frequent and doesn't create negative consequences. If they lose money, they'll chalk it up to having fun and won't try to gamble again in desperate attempts to win it back.

Compulsive gamblers, on the other hand, live to gamble. They're hooked on the rush they get from gambling. They fantasize about gambling, about winning big, and about ways to get money to gamble. They'll gamble on just about anything. Relationships with people become secondary. They'll spend rent and food money on lottery tickets or at a card game. In spite of how they hurt others, how ashamed and guilty they feel, they can't stop. For some, gambling becomes more important than life itself.

People with AD/HD are frequently drawn toward gambling because the thrill activates their brains. They not only feel good when they gamble, they become focused, energized, and alert. One study found that 50 percent of compulsive gamblers had a variant or difference in the dopamine receptor gene.[1] Treatment for compulsive gamblers can include the use of Naltraxon, a medication that blocks the rewarding effects of gambling. Naltraxon has been used for years to block the rewarding properties of heroin.

For those with AD/HD, combining their impulsiveness with the high they receive from gambling can result in a very serious addiction. When you picture a compulsive gambler, do you picture a man? Women become compulsive gamblers too. They do not usually gamble in the high-profile ways that men do, and women are less likely to be diagnosed or treated for this devastating addiction. Ali is a good example.

Almost Lost the Kids

Ali's father taught her to play poker when she was a girl. She knew how to bet and would frequently beat her dad's friends. She loved winning—not just the money, but the attention she got. Ali never did well in school, but she felt smart when she played cards. The more money riding on the game, the better she was able to focus.

Ali wouldn't normally put her two children in harm's way, yet she did. Her craving to gamble would override her judgment. She nearly lost custody of her kids when her six-year-old got scared and dialed 911; Ali had left her children home alone while she played cards next door.

SHOPPING

Spending money and buying things is part of life. But what if you can't control your spending? What if you buy things you don't need with money you don't have? That's when spending becomes a problem. Compulsive spenders buy because it feels good at the time and because the process is so absorbing that they can't think about anything else. The thrill of spending is short-lived, and the compulsive spender is left feeling shame and remorse. As with overeating, the buying is to soothe emotional pain or experience pleasure.

People with AD/HD are vulnerable to compulsive spending problems, especially because the impulsive quality of AD/HD makes it hard to think through the purchase. You see it. You want it. You buy it. Compulsive spending, like other addictions, leads to a variety of other problems, such as debt, poor credit, lying, guilt, and shame.

ADRENALINE JUNKIES

Another way to stimulate your AD/HD brain is by engaging in activities that increase adrenaline levels. Increased adrenaline activates the brain. Anyone can become addicted to adrenaline rushes from highly stimulating, or "high-stim," activities. High-stim activities such as bungee jumping, skydiving, and motor-cycle racing can be glamorous. Some people make a career out of them. Other high-stim behaviors, such as taking huge financial risks and traveling to war-torn parts of the world, are more subtle but can also be dangerous.

High-stim activities are especially attractive to certain people with AD/HD, providing the novelty and excitement their AD/HD brains crave. When an impulsive person seeks out these types of activities, the consequences can be dangerous, especially when you add alcohol or drugs to the mix.

Some people with AD/HD never lose their desire for high-stim activities. With treatment, however, they can have better judgment about the risks they take and use safety gear. Engaging in risky activities is always safer when you are not under the influence of drugs and alcohol. Many people who take AD/HD medication report that they snowboard, wind surf, or mountain bike better when they take their medication.

SEX AND LOVE ADDICTIONS

What turns sex and love into addictions is the same thing that turns spending into an addiction: loss of control. The ability to give and receive love is a joyous gift. Love truly is the answer to many of life's questions and dilemmas, but what if your feelings of love become obsessive? Is it possible to become addicted to a feeling such as love?

Absolutely. Love addiction occurs when you become dependent on, or addicted to, the love of another in order to feel a sense of self-worth or to be able to function in your daily life. Love addicts develop unrealistic or distorted perceptions of what love is and, like heroin junkies, are willing to sacrifice themselves in order to obtain what they mistakenly perceive as love.

Love addiction is characterized by obsessive thoughts about another person and compulsive behaviors, such as calling that person ten times a day. When you are addicted to love, you feel intense and relentless possessiveness, anger, fear of abandonment, jealousy, and other emotions. Not only do you feel these emotions deeply, you lose your ability to control your behavior and may act on these feelings. You disregard your own needs in your attempts to get an unrealistic type of love from another.

People with AD/HD are susceptible to becoming love addicts for several reasons:

- They may not have received the early bonding during infancy and childhood necessary to ensure a sense of security in adult relationships.
- Some people with AD/HD tend to feel worthless as a result of their disabilities. They spend their lives desperately seeking love and approval from others because they have such difficulty loving and approving of themselves.
- Children with AD/HD are at risk for physical, verbal, and sexual abuse. This abuse contributes to their willingness to sacrifice themselves for love and attention.

Sexual Addictions

Love and sex addictions frequently accompany each other, but they can also be separate problems. Our ability to be sexual and procreate is part of our humanness, but if we are unable to control our sexual impulses and desires, the consequences can be serious.

When it comes to sexuality, a person with AD/HD can have a low, average, or high sex drive. Some people with AD/HD constantly feel the need to express themselves sexually. Add poor impulse control to this need and you can see how sexual addiction might occur. This is not to say that everyone with a sexual addiction has AD/HD, only that some people with AD/HD are more vulnerable to sexual compulsivity than others.

Sex becomes an addiction when:

- You lose your ability to control your sexual behavior.
- You violate your moral, cultural, or religious values.
- You put yourself at risk to be physically, emotionally, and spiritually harmed.
- You risk exposure to sexually transmitted diseases and risk exposing others.
- You lie and are deceitful about your sexual behavior.

Some with AD/HD have sexual impulsively, especially if they are under the influence of alcohol and drugs. Others use sex as a way to stimulate their brain by taking risks. Voyeurs and exhibitionists can fall into this category. This is not to excuse sexual offenders or in any way to say that all those who offend have AD/HD. Poor impulse control combined with a drive toward high-risk behaviors can contribute to some with AD/HD becoming addicted to sex, or sexual acting out.

If you or someone you love has a sexual addiction, find a therapist or doctor who specializes in treating these disorders. There are also residential treatment programs that provide the intensive treatment that some sex and love addicts need. See appendix D for treatment centers, websites, and books that will provide you with resources.

Pornography

Compulsive use of pornography is a form of sexual addiction. The Internet provides an abundance of pornographic material, including paid sex with virtual partners, cybersex chat rooms, and online pornographic videos. The Internet is not the only place to view pornography, but it is the most common place. Internet companies make multimillions by offering and selling pornography. Men have a higher rate of overindulgence and addiction to porn, and it's especially seductive for men with AD/HD. Some men with serious AD/HD are not able to maintain relationships. These men often find their sexual release with pornographic material. It wasn't until several men with AD/HD revealed their "secret" to me that I began asking male clients with AD/HD about their sexual behavior. I was amazed at how many men with AD/HD have pornography and other sexual addictions. There are no statistics on the rate of pornography use among men with AD/HD, but I believe if the data was gathered, it would be shocking. People who suffer from these addictions are riddled with horrible feelings about themselves and are often self-medicating with food, alcohol, or drugs—piling one addiction on top of another, on top of their AD/HD. If you recognize yourself here, it's crucial for you to stop judging yourself and start talking to a professional who can help you with these addictions.

WORK ADDICTION

Work is good. It can provide us with a purpose, help others, enable us to express our talents, and help us to be financially responsible for ourselves and our families. But too much of a good thing can be harmful. The high energy and highly focused characteristics some people with AD/HD exhibit can predispose them to using work as a way to medicate their AD/HD restlessness, relationship difficulties, and need for constant stimulation. AD/HD difficulties such as organization, time management, prioritizing, and optimistically saying yes to more than is humanly possible can contribute to compulsive working. Problems with intimate relationships can also keep some at work when they could be at home.

Working for a Good Cause
Christa is devoted to her work with teenage runaways. She was an addicted adolescent who ran away from home when she was sixteen. At thirty-six, she has ten years in recovery, is married, and has a five-year-old son. Christa says that she has AD/HD, yet she has not received treatment for it. She will also joke about being a workaholic.

Christa's husband Roy has been angry about the sixty to seventy hours a week his wife works, especially since their son was born. Christa becomes so overfocused on her work that she doesn't realize the impact it is having on herself and her family. She feels guilty about spending so much time away from her family. When the weekend comes, Christa is often so exhausted that she spends most of it in bed. She fears that if she takes time off work, the fragile teen program that she started will fall apart.

Things came to a head when Christa spent most of the Thanksgiving holiday working and was too exhausted to be present when she was home. "I bet you can't stay away from work for three days," Roy had told her. "I can too," Christa bellowed defensively. But she couldn't. Christa came to a painful realization. "I'm addicted to my work. Even though it is hurting me and my family, I can't stop doing it." This was Christa's first step toward getting help for her work addiction.

EXERCISING TO EXHAUSTION

We know that exercise is good for us. It keeps our bodies healthy and improves our mental health. Exercise is especially important for those who have high-energy AD/HD, because it offers a healthy, constructive outlet for that energy. Aerobic exercise also increases levels of the neurotransmitters that give us a sense of well-being. However, even something as valuable as exercise can become an addiction.

Exercise may be an addiction when:

- You have difficulty functioning if you miss a day of exercise.
- You can't stop exercising, in spite of injuries.
- The amount and type of exercise you participate in harms your body.
- The amount of time spent exercising causes problems in other areas of your life, such as work, relationships, and physical health.
- Exercise is part of an unhealthy compulsion to lose weight.

Some people become so compulsive about exercise that they are not able to moderate themselves. Self-regulation is a huge problem for many with AD/HD and so is the concept of moderation. Some of us are either on or off. It's as though we need a dimmer switch to find other ways of being. The middle of the road may be the place you pass as your pendulum swings from one extreme to another. Many who compulsively exercise are afraid that if they miss a day they will not be able to stay with their routine. They may have had experience with this. This fear also compels them to exercise themselves into states of exhaustion or injury. If compulsive exercise is a problem for you, it's important to ask yourself whether this behavior is tied to an eating disorder.

WHAT TO DO?

If you realize that you're suffering from a behavioral addiction, now is the time to get help. You may want to contact a therapist or physician who has expertise in this area. Compulsive behaviors don't just disappear by themselves. You need help and support. Consider the resources mentioned in the appendices, as well as 12-step programs such as Gamblers Anonymous, Debtors Anonymous, Co-dependency Anonymous, Alanon, or Sex and Love Addicts Anonymous. Both your AD/HD and your behavioral addiction(s) must be treated in order for you to fully enjoy life.

After reading this far you may be wondering, "What else could possibly be wrong with me? I started out thinking or knowing that I have AD/HD and thinking that I overindulge, and now I identify with all sorts of problems." Try not to worry. Being aware that you have issues is the first step on the path of change. There may be things in your life that you have to address immediately. There are others you can deal with in time. We can't do it all at once. In the next chapter we will talk about the many attributes of people with AD/HD. Allow yourself to identify with these as well.

IT'S NOT ALL BAD

I WOULDN'T WISH AD/HD on anyone. It can make your life and the lives of those around you a living hell. Yet many with AD/HD have special talents and abilities along with the disabilities of the condition. You are far more than your disability.

Some people with physical, intellectual, or emotional disabilities have a tremendous capacity to adapt to life. Would they have the same level of courage and inner strength without the disability? We don't know for sure. People don't want to be disabled. However, many respond to the trauma of disability in amazing ways. They accept their disabilities as opportunities to grow and adapt, believing that the painful experience of being disabled allows them to develop a deeper sense of gratitude, meaning, and purpose.

Some people in 12-step programs talk about being "grateful" alcoholics or addicts. Who in their right mind would be grateful for suffering from the ravages of addiction? Most people are not grateful for the disabling, life-thrashing humiliation that eating disorders, substance disorders, and behavioral addictions bring into their lives. However, they are grateful for the joy, healing, adventure, self-exploration, spiritual awakening, and growth of recovery.

Not everyone in early recovery feels grateful to be clean and sober. Nor do some people who are new in Weight Watchers, Overeaters Anonymous, or treatment for their eating disorders.

Yet as they continue to recover, many feel the gratitude of not taking a drink or drug, or being obsessed with eating or not eating food. They are grateful to be released from bondage.

The same is true for AD/HD. No one expects you to jump up and down and say how grateful you are to have AD/HD. Yet with treatment, with time to heal and to practice new skills, you will be able to accept and appreciate the assets of having the brain style you do.

People with AD/HD have some great characteristics. These traits have not yet been clinically documented as having anything specifically to do with AD/HD, but I've witnessed them in hundreds of children and adults with amazing regularity. What you are about to read is not listed in most books or manuals as symptoms of AD/HD. Symptoms are problematic behaviors. Yet more and more experts in the field are talking and beginning to write about the common abilities and gifts of people with AD/HD.

TENACITY

Many people with AD/HD are tenacious, persistent, and determined. They can be like Energizer bunnies. They not only keep going, they find creative paths to get where they want to be. Some won't take "no" for an answer. Why do they keep trying, when "experts" have told them again and again that they're not "college material"? Or that the job of their dreams will never be within their reach?

These AD/HD folks have been told no since they were children, and from experience they learned that no doesn't mean no. It means try again, try harder, try something different. They found ways around, over, under, and through the obstacles. Some of us also have trouble with authority and will not accept "you can't do it." Your tenacity can become outright stubbornness. Yet there can be great rewards to being persistent.

I have a friend who wanted to publish a book about wedding planning. She sent her unsolicited book to eighty publishers. Most authors send a short book proposal that outlines what the book will be about, but not my friend. She sent the entire manuscript. After receiving her first dozen rejection letters, she started tossing her daily bundle of publisher letters unopened into a basket on her desk. It wasn't until one day when she started going through the basket that she found three offers from prominent publishers! Her book is in its third edition and has sold over 500,000 copies.

ADAPTABILITY

Tenacity alone is not enough. People with AD/HD develop and fine-tune skills that enable them to adapt to a world that doesn't always make sense to them. Their need to adapt can force them to develop abilities others may not have. I am constantly amazed at the brilliant adaptations people have made—even those who don't know they have AD/HD.

Entrepreneur by Default

Thom is a single parent of two children. After years of confining sales jobs, Thom found the job of his dreams. As program manager for a PC manufacturer, he worked in an innovative, laid-back corporate environment. He also worked as a life coach in the evenings.

Everything was great, but when things are too easy, the AD/HD brain gets bored and restless. Thom decided to get his MBA, while working full time and single parenting his children. After receiving his MBA, Thom found an even better job in a top software manufacturing company. The economy took a downturn, and many were laid off. Thom still had his job but was loaded with more technical tasks than he was hired for. It turned out to be an extremely harsh environment.

He was no longer thriving, but struggling to avoid getting laid off. About this time Thom was diagnosed with AD/HD and began taking medication. He was able to think and work more linearly. His newfound abilities, however, were not enough to protect him from the economy. Thom was laid off with thousands of other well-educated, well-paid professionals in Silicon Valley.

Life gave Thom no choice but to become an entrepreneur. This is a common scenario for many with AD/HD. Thom's experience helped him realize that he loved helping people and companies adapt to dramatic change. Today he is the founder of several companies that provide courses and consulting on personal and organizational change, as well as Internet business development. Thom is delighted with his ability to adapt and continually transform his life.

INTUITION

A highly developed ability to perceive the unspoken is frequently one of the helpful by-characteristics of AD/HD accommodation. The sense of intuition is similar to the senses of seeing, hearing, smelling, tasting, and feeling. It's your gut feeling. Because many people with AD/HD miss large portions of information and sensory input, they develop the ability to discern the big picture from the bits and pieces of the puzzle their brain latches on to. They often have great instinct. They can predict the next real-estate boom, know how to market products that have not yet been invented, and anticipate others' behavior. These abilities can lead to some very creative and lucrative careers.

Many people with AD/HD solve problems by using a combination of knowledge, divergent and creative thinking, and intuition. For example, the other day the smoke alarm in our living room began emitting a low-level screeching sound. Because the alarm is located at the peak of our open-beam ceiling, I asked my fourteen-year-old son Tyler to get the extension ladder from the garage. Instead he returned with a tennis ball. His first two shots missed, but the third was a direct hit and the screeching sound stopped. Tyler's AD/HD brain had quickly latched on to a quicker, more creative solution. The next day Tyler replaced the smoke alarm. This time he had to use the ladder.

Sometimes we know things just because we know them. If you have AD/HD, you may possess ideas, information, and truths you can't explain. But having the correct answer is not always enough; your teacher, spouse, or employer may be more interested in the steps you took to get there. It is often quite difficult for people with AD/HD to explain their conclusions, because they may not understand the process that got them there. Their brains work quickly and from all directions at once. This makes the linear backtracking necessary for a scientific explanation next to impossible. When your boss asks how you came to a decision, the answer "I don't know" or "It just felt right" doesn't cut it, but it may be all you have.

While a highly developed intuition is valuable, we can get ourselves into trouble if we rely on it too much. The ability to think and live in a linear fashion is crucial to functioning in our world. While linear thinking differs from creative thinking, both are needed if individuals are to be competent in society.

UNCENSORED HONESTY

Over the years, I've met many people with AD/HD who are honest to the core. They tell you the truth about everything, partially because they don't have the ability to censor. Whatever they think, they say. This type of honesty can be valuable and endearing. There are some people with AD/HD who are loyal and incredibly trustworthy. They have a level of honesty that goes beyond answering questions truthfully. They will openly share their innermost feelings and thoughts. They tend to tell people personal information that is often helpful to others and creates rich bonds. Their honesty is refreshing and people are attracted to them. They have the ability to forge great friendships.

The flip side of uncensored honesty is brutal truthfulness. Just because something is true doesn't mean you always have to be the messenger. I wonder if the child in the fable who blurted, "The emperor has no clothes," was blessed with the uncensored honesty of childhood or if his statement was a result of his AD/HD. After all, none of the other people at the emperor's parade told the truth about what they really saw; yet this child couldn't help telling the truth.

People with uncensored honesty often reveal intimate details about their lives in situations that are not to their advantage. By doing so, they expose themselves to the negative scrutiny of others. Learning to assess a situation and regulate impulses to tell the truth, the whole truth, and nothing but the truth are highly valuable skills.

DIVERGENT AND EXPANSIVE THINKING

Divergent thinking is unique and uncharacteristic of standard linear thinking. It is also expansive, elastic, extensive, sweeping, and comprehensive. Divergent thinkers are able to answer a question or solve a problem by accessing a plethora of information and possibilities. They're able to quickly sift through massive amounts of information from a variety of sources and find unique and creative ideas. This type of thinking and processing is immensely valuable in many professions.

Thinking Outside the Box

What box? The problem for some of us is that we never knew there was a box we were supposed to be thinking in. This may have caused you pain when you were in linear situations such as school.

As with many things in life, the same trait can be both a problem and a blessing. Divergent and expansive thinking can be invaluable one moment and disabling the next. Some people find careers where their thinking style is essential to the work environment and greatly appreciated, such as advertising and marketing. Their minds are able to expand in all directions and return with bits and pieces of seemingly unrelated ideas. Then they integrate these thoughts, adding fresh twists to create unique images and ideas. Often those with AD/HD are extremely valuable in brainstorming sessions.

Finding a compatible work environment that makes use of your thinking style can make a huge difference in your life. Some experts speculate that Walt Disney, Thomas Edison, Frank Lloyd Wright, Albert Einstein, and Henry Ford had AD/HD. Many innovative computer start-up companies are staffed with AD/HD visionaries. With good secretarial and clerical support, these men and women are exceptional in their careers. Unfortunately, many experience problems with substance abuse, relationships, and self-esteem related to their AD/HD, in spite of their business success.

CREATIVITY

Creativity is an experience and expression of energy. It is the ability to cause something to exist, yet it is more than the end product of a poem, photograph, garden, marketing campaign, song, or dance. Creativity is the internal energy we are born with that enables us to express our thoughts, feelings, and experiences in our own unique way.

Many people with AD/HD are highly creative. I've worked with an unusual number of clients who play music, paint, sculpt, or write. Others are photographers, videographers, visionaries, inventors, architects, seamstresses, mechanics, and parents.

Physicist Albert Einstein said, "Imagination is more important than knowledge." I believe that many people with AD/HD have heightened creativity because they can best express themselves in divergent and expansive ways. The gift of creativity gives people ways to express themselves in nonacademic, less linear, and untraditional ways.

The Blessing and the Curse

We are all born with creative energy that demands expression. But children learn early in life that coloring outside the lines is wrong, that trees are not red and the sky is not green. In time, they learn that doing it like everyone else gets the best reactions from the people they want to please. What happens to creative energy? Does it just go away? No, it needs an outlet, just as does physical, emotional, sexual, spiritual, and intellectual energy.

Without expression, creative energy implodes, or blows up inside us. Imploded energy of any type can lead to depression, physical and emotional illness, discontentment, and restlessness.

The blessing of highly developed creativity is often accompanied by the curse of having to express it. If the child with AD/HD continues to draw red trees no matter what others think, she may be able to salvage and express that creative part of herself. But if she can't find ways to express her imagination, she becomes frustrated. Children like her are described as having "too much" energy, imagination, and impulsivity, and not enough logic, attention, seriousness, and socialization.

People with AD/HD may deal with their frustration by drowning it with alcohol, numbing it with drugs, or stuffing it with food. If you are wired for creative expression, it's important to honor that about yourself. Find ways to create whatever your heart desires. The process of creating, not the outcome, is the important thing. You don't have to make a career out of expressing your creativity, just do it. You and the people in your life will feel better for the effort.

SENSE OF HUMOR

Several of the funniest people I know have AD/HD, and I don't think it's a coincidence. The combination of a quick wit and the ability to laugh at themselves and life makes them fun to be around. Some psychologists say humor can be a defense mechanism against other feelings such as sadness, anger, embarrassment, or pain, and this is true in some cases. Why not take a defense mechanism and turn it into an art form? Years of feeling different, angry, sad, and ashamed take their toll. Many with AD/HD take the lemons life throws at them and laugh while they juggle.

If you've ever been to a 12-step meeting or other recovery group, you may have been surprised by the laughter you heard. People are struggling with serious problems that have devastated their lives. Not everyone in recovery feels joyous and filled with merriment, yet there is often a lighthearted atmosphere of humor and laughter when recovering people get together.

I've observed over the years how alcoholics, addicts, and people with AD/HD in particular utilize the healing properties of laughter. The shame and humiliation of addictions and AD/HD are reduced by expressing the ironic and funny aspects of both. Their humor can be quick, tangential, poignant, understated, and brilliant in its simplicity.

In no way do I want to minimize the seriousness and profound impact AD/HD has on your life. You may not have AD/HD, but still experience the pain and frustration of loving someone who does. You may struggle with your AD/HD every day, and yet identify with some of the attributes and assets discussed in this chapter—tenacity, creativity, humor, honesty, and divergent thinking. Hold on to the qualities and gifts you have, and remember you are more than a disorder.

CHANGE YOUR BEHAVIOR, CHANGE YOUR LIFE

tools
to help
you
adapt
and thrive

THERE ARE NUMEROUS WAYS to survive and thrive with AD/HD, whether or not you take medication. They all involve learning different behaviors and coping skills that minimize the negative effects of AD/HD and maximize your assets. The tools we're going to discuss in this chapter are not meant to be a substitute for medication. It's hard to build a house with just building materials, a hammer, and nails if there's no foundation to build upon, and for some, medication will provide the foundation on which to build a different life. In addition, I don't suggest you try everything in this chapter as a way to avoid taking medication. Once you're diagnosed with AD/HD, it's important to consider what your health-care provider suggests in the context of your life. We'll look at some of the specific problems related to AD/HD, such as issues of personal boundaries, communication style, self-care skills, and the role of an AD/HD coach.

Regardless of whether your treatment plan includes medication, you'll want to think about these various ways to enhance your quality of life. First though, let's look at your own potential for making changes in your life.

THE COMPONENTS OF CHANGE

In order to make changes in your life, you'll probably want to start by recognizing what it takes to accomplish your goals. I like to break it down into the five basic components involved in making changes: awareness, willingness, tools, practice, and patience.

Awareness

First, we have to be aware there is something we need to change in our life. Self-awareness can be difficult for people with AD/HD, but because you're reading this book, you're ahead of the game. Sometimes people with AD/HD are surprised and embarrassed to find out how their behavior affects others. They are often unaware of the specific behaviors that keep them stuck in patterns that don't serve them well. If you are not aware that you have a problem, there is no reason for you to make changes. For example, you may be aware that you have gained weight, yet not connect it to the fact that you are overeating, or you may deny that your weight gain bothers you, hence you see no problem.

Willingness

Why are some people willing to sacrifice and work hard to change and others aren't? Motivation usually comes from pain and the desire to stop hurting. This is especially true when we self-medicate AD/HD with alcohol, food, and drugs. Initially it works. But inevitably self-medicating stops working, and the one-time solution is now a problem of its own. Now we have two sources of pain rousing us to take action.

When the pain becomes intolerable, some of us become willing to change. Willingness means moving from acceptance of your behavior to a realization that it's not okay. Your behavior has to bother you enough that you're finally prepared to do the work to change.

"Because It Bothers You"

My friend Jim grew up with an alcoholic mother and father. His brother was also an alcoholic, as were many of his friends. Jim was a successful businessman who had numerous accounts on two continents, but his alcoholism progressed to the point that he would wake up on the beach in his own vomit. His life had narrowed to drinking on the sofa in his one room apartment.

Jim went to his family doctor because he knew he had to stop drinking. "But why?" he wondered. "My father, my brother, and most of my friends drink. Why do I have to quit?" The doctor responded, "Because it bothers you." It bothered Jim to act the way he did when he drank. His deteriorating lifestyle bothered him. It bothered him that he couldn't control his drinking. Once Jim realized how much he hated his life, his willingness to change followed. At the time of this writing, Jim hasn't had a drink in over twenty-five years, and actively helps others to get and stay sober.

Tools

Once we become willing, we need tools to help us change. Most of us need help to stop overeating, drinking, gambling, or sexually acting out. How many times have you tried to stop, only to start again? Have you ever resolved to change your behavior through willpower alone and found that it just doesn't work? Now is the time to look at the resources available and decide where to start. Here are some options:

- Therapists, psychologists, and doctors with expertise in AD/HD and/or addiction
- Support groups like 12-step programs, after-care groups, or group counseling
- Education about AD/HD and addictions through books, CDs, the Internet, and workshops
- A support person from your network of friends, family, coworkers, or neighbors, or your church
- Inpatient programs for situations more severe and long-standing

Practice

It takes major effort to recover from AD/HD and addictions. When you are practicing something new, you will make mistakes. Give yourself the grace to slip up, but don't give up. Remember that you are a work in progress.

As you begin to integrate new skills, behaviors, and ways of coping, and practice them over and over, they'll start to become routine. Pretty soon they'll be almost second nature. Change is something you make day by day. Practice doesn't mean perfection, practice means progress.

Patience

The final piece of effective and lasting change is patience—a virtue that most people with AD/HD find challenging. It has taken you a lifetime to get to where you are today, and it will take long-term growth and change to heal. Please be patient with yourself.

Remember that it is your lifetime, no one else's. You are on your own schedule of healing.

If you're quitting an addiction and changing your AD/HD behavior, it's natural to want to see immediate results. Some days you'll notice progress, and other days it will feel like "one step forward, two steps back." That's normal!

Patience may be difficult but it's crucial to your success. Recovery is not a race, and you don't have to compare yourself to how fast or graceful others may appear. Recovery is your new way of living.

Now that we've looked at five basic components of change, let's get into specific strategies for improving your life of AD/HD and addiction. The important thing is to make sure you're getting your basic needs met.

MEETING YOUR BASIC NEEDS

Here is another place where AD/HD and addictions overlap. Some people with AD/HD can function at high levels, yet have trouble meeting their basic needs. People with eating disorders or substance and behavioral addictions, even those in recovery, have many of the same issues of self-regulating their basic functions.

The good news is that you will notice improvement by taking some fairly simple steps. There is a saying in AA known as the HALT principle: Don't get too Hungry, Angry, Lonely, or Tired. I'd like to add two more elements: Excitable and Dehydrated. These are all situations that make both AD/HD and addiction recovery difficult. If you're in recovery and you sink into these conditions, you're liable to be HALTED—stopped! Let's look at each element of HALTED in more detail.

Hungry

Being hungry makes you susceptible to giving in to your addictions, and doesn't help your AD/HD behaviors. It's common for people with AD/HD to have difficulties keeping their brain fed. Our brain works well when it has a consistent supply of nutritious food, and most people are aware of feeling crummy if it's been too long between meals. Yet some people with AD/HD have a hard time pulling themselves away from what they are doing to take time to eat. Others will make lunch and forget to eat it. There are also those who snack all day, but they are eating food that doesn't enhance their brain functioning.

It takes concerted effort to feed your body properly and avoid excessive hunger. Planning ahead, making lists, and shopping regularly may not come easily for you. Try starting your day with a breakfast of protein, such as eggs, milk, cheese, and meats, to help your brain function at an optimal level. (D. Steven Ledingham, author of *The Scoutmaster's Guide to Attention Deficit Disorder*, suggests to parents of children with AD/HD that they give their children lunch or dinner foods for breakfast.[1]) Keep nutritious snacks available—at home, at work, even in your car. Try to eat as soon as you feel hungry. That "starved" feeling can lead to impulsive choices, such as eating food high in sugar and carbohydrates.

Angry

Of course you're angry. Who wouldn't be? You never asked to have AD/HD, eating disorders, or addictions. Anger can be a defense against feeling powerless to control your situation. But if you don't deal with anger, it turns into resentment, which eats away at you and erodes your self-esteem and happiness. If you let yourself get too angry, too often, you'll be more vulnerable to your addictive behaviors and less able to change your AD/HD tendencies. The goal is to find ways to release anger and avoid getting stuck in it.

It's easier for some of us to be angry about a situation than to do something to change it. Eleanor Roosevelt summed it up by saying, "It's better to light a candle than curse the darkness." The way to work through anger is first to acknowledge that you are angry. You are not just bothered or irritated, you are angry. Once you've accepted your anger, you can find healthy ways of expressing it.

You might talk with a trusted friend or counselor about your angry feelings. This may help you decide if and how you might address the person you are angry with. Later in this chapter, we will talk about assertive ways to resolve conflict. You may find that your anger is directed at a work relationship or living situation. It is helpful to look at accepting the things you cannot change, changing the things you can, and asking for the wisdom and willingness to know the difference.

Some people need to express their anger physically by running, working out, martial arts, or digging a garden. For many, verbal and physical expression combined with acceptance can keep anger from turning into resentment.

Lonely

Feeling connected with others is a basic human need. It's essential to be a part of a family, neighborhood, workplace, school, and group of friends. But people often isolate themselves when they're tired, depressed, embarrassed, or ashamed. They don't want others to see them because they view themselves so poorly. When we isolate ourselves, we're at the mercy of whatever our brain tells us, and it's not always nice. If we detach from others, we miss out on their love, their energy, and the positive regard they have for us.

Frequently it isn't until people get treatment that they realize how lonely they are. Drugs, alcohol, and/or food have become their primary relationship. Joining support groups and 12-step programs can help people meet new friends. Taking a night course or joining a dance class, a bowling league, or a gardening club can lead to positive connections with other like-minded people. Twenty-one-year-old Zach was afraid that if he quit drinking, he'd never have fun again. "So here I am now with all these clean and sober friends, having fun and not drinking. I never would have believed I'd be doing this."

Loneliness makes us vulnerable to the exact behaviors we're trying to change. Taking concrete action to nurture positive relationships goes a long way toward helping us get and stay healthy.

Tired

Sleep problems are a core symptom for approximately 70 percent of adults with AD/HD.[2] Chronic sleep deprivation hampers daytime alertness, impairs memory, and reduces the ability to think and process information. It also decreases attention. These are already problems for the person with AD/HD; lack of sleep makes all of these troubles worse.

Becoming aware that you're sleep deprived is the first step in working on getting better sleep. Some sleep solutions are discussed in chapter 6. Many other resources are available to help with sleep, including books, relaxation exercises, doctors, and clinics. Enter "sleep disorder" into any Internet search engine to get started on your search for help.

Excitable

It's easy to get overstimulated, agitated, and all stirred up over the smallest things. The AD/HD brain can seek conflict, provoke others, and create drama without being aware of it. If you're going to stop your addictions, you're going to have to live a life compatible with recovery. There's no payoff to getting irritated, frantic, and frenetic—you don't get to self-medicate.

Be aware of situations in which you become excitable. Learn to remove yourself from a potentially volatile situation or calm yourself in the midst of one. There may be people in your life who constantly create drama and crisis. Excitability is contagious, so ask yourself if their energy is good for you. Over time, you may choose to be with people who are fascinating, funny, and outrageous at times, and yet have an overall calm and stable approach to life.

Dehydrated

You may be picturing someone with cracked lips crawling over dry, parched sands in the desert. That's not what I'm talking about. Many of us don't get enough fluids. Your body and brain need water for optimal functioning. Caffeinated drinks contribute to the problem, acting as a diuretic and causing you to excrete fluids from your body. Many sodas have preservatives like sodium benzoate, which even in small amounts can make you thirsty. Alcohol is the worst dehydrator, which is why people with a hangover are usually very thirsty.

Practice paying attention to your body and recognizing when you need to drink water. You can increase your water intake by having water bottles in your car, at work, and at home. Seeing water bottles will remind you to drink water. Think water before you go to the fridge or store, or order a drink with your meal.

| | | | | |

As you are incorporating strategies to meet your basic needs, you can also look at some other areas of life that you might want to improve. We'll start with communication.

COMMUNICATION

One of the most important aspects of a healthy life is positive and effective communication with those around us. Unfortunately, communication can be heavily impacted by AD/HD and further hampered by addictions. I like to break down communication into four categories: listening, conversing, resolving conflict, and making true amends. These activities overlap but it's helpful to look at them separately.

Listening and Hearing

Active listening is an art. However, many people with AD/HD are masters of another dangerous art: listening without hearing. People in your life get upset when they find out you really didn't hear what they said; otherwise, you wouldn't have asked how their mother was when they've just told you about her cancer. When people aren't heard, they feel that what they are saying isn't important to you. Here are some suggestions to improve your listening skills.

- Practice becoming aware when you are in an "uh huh" or head-nodding trance.
- When you realize you're not listening, refocus on the speaker. They may be giving you valuable information, but your attention is turned off.
- Ask questions about information you have missed or anything you're not sure you heard correctly.
- When you're interacting with people, mute the television, put down the newspaper, or turn off the radio.
- Stay engaged by participating in the conversation without dominating.

Conversation

Many with AD/HD have trouble carrying on balanced conversations. Their mind may wander, keeping them from actively listening. They may be too talkative and tend to dominate a discussion. They may have learned to say very little for fear of saying too much. They may also be afraid of their own tendency to reveal too much about themselves. Here are a few tips for improving your conversational skills.

- Recognize when you feel rushed to end conversations. Take a deep breath; ask yourself if you really need to hurry.
- If someone says something that upsets you, stop and allow yourself to think before you respond.
- Try not to take another person's mood personally. It's usually more about that person than you.
- If you find yourself having trouble keeping a conversation going, ask questions. People love to talk about themselves, and it's the easiest way to stay engaged.

- If you're speaking rapidly or excitedly, remind yourself to stop and take a breath or two. Give the other person a chance to talk.

Resolving Conflict

Conflict is a natural consequence of human interaction. There are three primary ways to deal with conflicts: being passive, assertive, or aggressive. The conflict resolution continuum shows each style and the associated behaviors.

STYLES OF CONFLICT RESOLUTION

PASSIVE	ASSERTIVE	AGGRESSIVE
■ Solves conflict by giving in	■ Asks for needs directly	■ Sacrifices others
■ Sacrifices self	■ Communicates	■ Shames
■ Feels unentitled	■ Cooperates	■ Blames
■ Disregards own needs	■ Negotiates	■ Intimidates
	■ Respects self and others	■ Disregards others' needs

We learn to solve conflicts by watching those around us. If you grew up in a family where angry words were rarely spoken, chances are there was a lot of unexpressed anger floating around your home. You had no role models to show you how people deal constructively with conflict. You may have developed a passive style of conflict resolution, or you may try to avoid conflict at all costs. Solving conflict by being passive means that you sacrifice yourself.

On the other hand, if you grew up in a family where arguing was the norm, you may meet conflict with aggression. Some people with AD/HD seek conflict. Fights with others stimulate their brain. The energy produced by the conflict is painful but it's also activating. Aggressive behavior is rarely an effective way to handle conflict. The needs of others are sacrificed, and relationships are damaged and even lost.

Being assertive when dealing with conflict means that you neither sacrifice your needs or those of the other person. This takes communicating, cooperating, and negotiating.

The Vegetarian and the Carnivore

Let's use the example of you and a friend deciding where to go for dinner. You are a vegetarian and your friend enjoys a good steak. Your friend asks, "Would you like to go to the steak house on Ocean Street?" You realize the restaurant doesn't have a salad bar, or much else for non-meat eaters. You may be so used to sacrificing your needs that you don't remind your friend that you don't eat meat, and you say, "Okay." Meanwhile, you're stewing all the way to dinner. You are preoccupied trying to convince yourself that it will be okay. Your friend has no idea that you aren't happy about the decision, and you end up feeling resentful as you sit in the restaurant eating your baked potato. The passive approach sacrifices your own needs and doesn't enhance the relationship.

An aggressive response to the same dinner question could go something like this:

"Would you like to go to the steak house for dinner?"

"No!! Did you forget that I don't eat meat, or do you just not care? What a stupid idea! Take a vegetarian to a red meat factory for dinner! Sheesh! We're going to Veggie Palace."

You not only state your demands, you shame the other person. You leave no room for communicating, cooperating, or negotiating. You may have gotten your way this time, but there may not be another time. Your friend may find another dinner partner.

Being assertive is somewhere in between. Again the question, "Would you like to go to the steakhouse?"

The assertive response: "Not really. I don't eat meat and the steakhouse doesn't offer much else. Is there another place that has good steak along with some vegetarian dishes or a salad bar?" By communicating your desires and posing the question to your friend, you have set the stage for more communication. If your friend responds from an assertive place, the dialogue might go something like this:

"I forgot you don't eat meat. What if we go to the Crow's Nest," your friend suggests. "They have a salad bar and I love the steak."

"Great idea." And off you go to dinner.

You clearly communicated your preference, and you and your friend were able to cooperate and negotiate, creating a win-win situation. This can bring you and your friend closer as you learn more about each other.

Making True Amends

Do you feel like you do and say things that are hurtful to others, even when you don't mean to? Welcome to the world of AD/HD. We say too much or too little, or speak in such circular ways that even we get lost. No wonder so many people with AD/HD are misunderstood and misinterpreted.

Some with AD/HD can come across as offensive and/or defensive. People with AD/HD are especially inclined to defend or explain their actions. Of course, there are times when it's essential to explain your actions so that others understand you. But the person with AD/HD can take it to such an extreme that the receiver may feel overloaded with information that is distracting and confusing.

It's not enough to say, "I'm sorry." In fact, many with AD/HD have said it so much throughout their lives that it has become meaningless and may actually inflame the receiver who has heard it one too many times. Try practicing the three A's: Acknowledge, Apologize, and Amend.

The Three A's

Acknowledge: Take responsibility for what you did or said. Don't blame others or get into explanations. Pay attention to your own actions, not those of others. "Yes, I was disrespectful to you when I told you I'd get right off the computer and come to dinner. I let myself get caught up and you had to ask me several times." Once you begin to accept that being wrong is part of being human, it's easier to admit.

Apologize: In order to give a clear meaningful apology, you have to understand what you did. This is why the generic "I'm sorry" holds so little value. Think about how the other person feels. Ask clarifying questions if you really don't understand how you contributed to the problem. If you were wrong, say so, and give a sincere apology. "I was wrong to act that way. I apologize for hurting your feelings."

Amend: This is where you take action to make things better when you can. You write an apology letter or talk directly with the person you harmed. You let the other person know that you will work to avoid repeating what you did or said that hurt him or her. Then ask, "Is there anything else I can do to make this better?"

People in your life will feel relief when you admit that what you did was wrong, apologize for the upset your actions caused, and are willing to change your behavior.

| | | | | |

Healthy communication leads to stronger and more positive relationships with others. Another way to maintain your relationships is to understand appropriate boundaries.

BOUNDARIES

A boundary is something that marks a border or a limit. In psychological terms, a physical boundary is the space around each of us that we feel uncomfortable allowing others to enter. Have you ever had someone talk inches from your face or hug or kiss you, and you felt uncomfortable? That person invaded your "personal space." He or she didn't respect your physical boundaries. What would feel fine coming from your spouse or your child may feel awful coming from someone with whom you're not close.

Likewise, we all have emotional boundaries that vary according to the closeness of the relationship. When a stranger asks you personal questions, or a casual acquaintance dumps his or her problems on you, you may feel your emotional boundaries have been violated. The relationship was not intimate enough to support that level of interaction. We all have comfort levels regarding how close we like others to get.

Emotional boundaries are like a series of circular fences, one inside the other, each with its own gates. We let certain people through the gates, from the outside in, depending on the situation and our level of comfort. We select the people we let in and how far we let them in, just as we choose who we will keep at a distance. Sometimes our fences are falling down in places and almost anyone can walk in or trample over. Or we have built fences with barbed wire and no gates so that no one can get close to us. Healthy boundaries are those that we control. Our fences are solid and sturdy yet have many gates that we can open to let people into our emotional life.

Boundaries, AD/HD, and Addictions
People with AD/HD seem to consistently struggle with maintaining their own boundaries and not violating the boundaries of others. Their impulsiveness causes them to disclose more about themselves than is good for them. Some are used to being pushy, dominating, and controlling just to get through life. Most

Boundaries

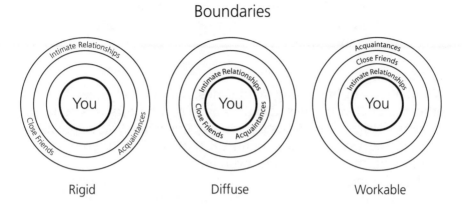

Rigid   Diffuse   Workable

people with AD/HD don't mean to be intrusive or disrespectful. They often don't realize when they've violated another's boundaries or allowed someone to violate their own. Some have such strong personalities that others are afraid to tell them how they come across. Without feedback, it's hard for them to change their behavior.

Let's look at some specific boundary difficulties you may have and explore changes that can help you improve your relationships.

Knowing When It's Time to Leave

Do you stay in relationships, jobs, and living situations long after their value is gone? Knowing when to leave is important. Many people with AD/HD do not pick up on subtle or even blatant cues to move on. People with AD/HD may stay in relationships too long because of difficulty dealing with change and an inability to discern when the relationship is no longer viable. People also stay in all types of situations because they don't know how to be assertive. Here are a few ideas to consider.

- When spending time with others, pay attention to cues such as yawning and watch-peeking that lets you know it's time to go.
- If you are unhappy in a job or relationship, consider your options. Staying may not be your only option.
- Consider setting time limits. "If my relationship isn't improving in three to six months, I will talk about moving on."

- Ask yourself, "Is this the job, relationship, living space, or social or business event where I really want to spend my precious time?"

Just Say No

We all have trouble saying no at times. It's nice to help and please others, but if you have AD/HD you may take this desire to the extreme. How many times do you say *yes* when you really mean *no*? Do the words "Sure, I can do that" fly out of your mouth before you know what "that" even is?

Developing the ability to say no will give you more control over your life, and will also decrease your resentment toward others. Keep in mind that people in your life may not always react positively to behavioral changes, especially if the changes affect them. Be aware, but don't let it stop you from taking care of yourself.

Here are some tips to help you say no when you need to:

- Accept that, like everybody else, you have limits.
- Consider letting callers leave messages rather than answering the phone. This can give you time to think before you call back.
- If someone is asking you in person, say you'll think about it and will get back to him or her as soon as possible.
- Think the situation through. Do you really have time to make six dozen cookies?
- The best way to decline is short and kind: "I've checked my calendar and I'm not going to be able to help you move next weekend." You don't have to explain why.
- It's okay to change your mind and say, "I'm sorry, but now that I've thought about it, I realize I can't go to the movies tonight."
- Remember—you were not put on this planet to do everything for everyone! Cut yourself some slack when your inner critic tells you that you "should" do this or that.

| | | | | |

Learning to respect boundaries—your own and others'—is an important step in managing your AD/HD behavior. However, it's not always easy, and you may find you need help. One option is to utilize an AD/HD coach.

AD/HD COACHING

As more adults look for ways to thrive with their AD/HD, more resources are becoming available. Coaching is one resource that can be life-changing. A coach is not an alternative to a therapist or counselor. A coach can be a great adjunct to therapy and valuable if you don't need therapy.

Coaches help their clients understand how AD/HD impacts their lives and the lives of those around them. The coach's job is to sensitively point out styles and strategies that haven't served the client well. They aid their clients in making changes by providing structure and accountability, and helping the clients set and attain goals. Some people with AD/HD initially need help getting enough sleep, eating regularly, taking their medication, and getting to appointments on time. Others use their coach to excel in their school or career.

Coaches are generally very practical and centered on behavior (unlike a therapist or psychologist, who may be more focused on the internal thoughts and feelings behind behavior). Having someone to talk with who understands and is not judgmental can be a healing experience and a first for many. In some cases the relationship with the coach gives the client the confidence to have more personal relationships. Most importantly, coaches provide their clients with hope and tools to create a better life.

Professional coaches know their boundaries. They know that they are not acting as a doctor, psychologist, social worker, or therapist, even though some coaches have degrees and licenses in these professions. Coaches shouldn't act as your realtor, landlord, or business partner, and should never develop a romantic relationship with you. As of this writing there is no standardized credential or licensure for coaches. There are reputable training and certificate programs for coaches, but there are also individuals who just decide they are coaches. The Attention Deficit Disorder Association (ADDA), the largest national adult AD/HD organization, created the *ADDA Guiding Principles for Coaching Individuals with Attention Deficit Disorder*, which you can find at www.add.org.

Here are some tips for finding a reputable coach:

- Ask your doctor, therapist, and friends for recommendations.
- Ask the coach about his or her training and credentials.

- Find a coach who specializes in coaching clients with AD/HD.
- Ask about the terms of your work together. This includes cost, scheduling, length of sessions, and whether you'll meet in person, by phone, or via the Internet. Coaches charge by the month, week, or hour. The hourly fee is between $50 and $200.
- Ask about the coach's confidentiality policy. All information should be held in strict confidence unless you sign a release of information.
- Ask if your coach is willing to work with other members of your treatment team.

KEEPING AN OPEN MIND

I hope this chapter has provided you with information and ideas that will help you manage your AD/HD. People have varying degrees of AD/HD and are impacted in unique ways during different stages of their lives. It may not be enough to change your thinking, emotions, and behavior. You may need to have your AD/HD treated at the biological level.

The next chapter will give you an overview of medication options. You will be the one to decide if taking medication is right for you. Keep in mind that medication is not "the last resort." Rather, it's one more tool in your tool belt. Some of us need more tools than others.

THE TRUTH ABOUT MEDICATION

how, why, and when it may be right for you

BECAUSE I AM NOT a doctor, for assistance I turned to my friend Dwaine McCallon, MD, a gifted physician with years of experience treating children, adults, and prison inmates with AD/HD. My colleague Richard Gilbert, MD, a psychiatrist with extensive expertise in treating AD/HD in children and adults, also provided information and clarity about medications used to treat AD/HD and its many co-occurring conditions.

Treating adults and children with medication has been, and continues to be, the subject of great controversy. Even after years of scientific research, advances in understanding how these medications work, and significant improvement in the quality of life for millions around the world, there are still those who question the role that medication provides in the treatment of AD/HD. Even more controversial is treating recovering alcoholics and addicts with psychostimulant medication.

The media has targeted the "evils" of Ritalin for years. Fear and lack of accurate information fuel anti-Ritalin and anti-medication groups. No wonder recovering alcoholics and addicts, treatment professionals, and members of 12-step programs have been slow to embrace the use of stimulant medication to treat AD/HD in those with co-occurring addictions.

Journals and popular magazines have recently been providing more accurate and scientific information on medications to treat AD/HD. Unbiased information based on sound research with proven results diminishes fear of the unknown and squelches myths about the effective use of medication to treat AD/HD.

- Untreated AD/HD is a risk factor for developing a substance use disorder later in life.[1]
- The more co-occurring conditions a person with AD/HD has, the greater the risk for substance use disorders.[2]
- Treating AD/HD with stimulant medication reduces the risk of later substance use disorders by 50 percent.[3]
- Treating AD/HD in children and adolescents with stimulants has a greater protective effect for youth than adults in regard to future substance use disorders.[4]
- In children and adults with correctly diagnosed AD/HD, some medication will be effective about 80 percent of the time.[5]

THE BOTTOM LINE

People with AD/HD can benefit from some of the non-medical approaches mentioned in previous chapters. For some, however, medication is essential if they are to stay sober and out of jails and institutions. They are biologically incapable of controlling the impulses that can lead to impulsive criminal behavior and addiction relapse. Research shows that children who had their AD/HD treated with stimulant medication actually have less risk of substance abuse than those who were not medicated.[6]

Psychostimulant medications, when properly prescribed and monitored, are effective for approximately 75-80 percent of people with AD/HD.[7] These medications include stimulants such as Ritalin, Metadate, Focalin Concerta, Dexedrine, and Adderall. Nonstimulant medications such as Wellbutrin and Strattera are also effective for treating AD/HD symptoms in many individuals. We will discuss medications used to treat the many co-occurring conditions of AD/HD in detail later in this chapter.

MEDICATION IN RECOVERY

Recovering alcoholics and addicts are not flocking to doctors to get medication to treat their AD/HD. Many are hesitant (for good reason) to use medication, especially psychostimulants. It has been my experience that individuals in recovery become willing to try medication when they understand the potential benefit and the low potential for abuse. The chance of abusing medication is low when a comprehensive treatment program is in place.

Comprehensive Treatment

A comprehensive treatment plan is the most effective way to avoid medication abuse or addiction relapse. *Medication should not be used as the sole treatment for AD/HD.* Taking pills to rebalance your neurotransmitters is not enough. Your AD/HD and other co-occurring conditions must be treated as well. If you stray away from your addiction recovery, you will be at greater risk for relapse. If you don't receive adequate treatment for your AD/HD, you're at greater risk for relapse. A comprehensive treatment plan is one that contains the following components:

- AD/HD treatment in the form of education, coaching, and support groups
- Regular visits with your doctor and close medication management
- Therapy or counseling regarding AD/HD and recovery issues
- Involvement in addiction recovery programs
- Family and relationship counseling when needed
- Concurrent treatment for coexisting conditions if they are present (bipolar, eating disorders, anxiety disorders, obsessive thought patterns)

Not everyone has the resources to get all of the above services. The bare minimum would be active involvement in addiction recovery such as 12-step programs, working with a sponsor who can support your AD/HD recovery, and close medication management from your doctor.

Those with histories of substance abuse may prefer to use nonstimulant medication. This is a good idea in that it eliminates the potential for abuse or addiction. This does not, however, mean that people in recovery should not use stimulant medication. It depends on the individual and his or her stage of recovery, support system, level of honesty, and willingness to comply with treatment. It is important to remember that your drug abuse may have been an effort to self-medicate conditions you have had for a long time.

WHY AND WHEN IT MAY BE RIGHT FOR YOU

Whether or not you decide to treat your AD/HD with medication is a difficult decision. You may be thinking, "Drugs almost killed me. I've spent years trying to get off them, and now you want me to start taking them?" I know. At first it sounds pretty crazy, but bear with me as I explain why medication can help. Remember, it's your decision. People in recovery should be extremely cautious when taking medications in general, but being cautious doesn't necessarily mean abstaining from all prescribed medications.

If you are a member of a 12-step group, you may hear people at meetings say, "You just don't take anything, no matter what." You may also have a sponsor who doesn't support the use of medication to treat emotional and medical problems. However, Alcoholics Anonymous has become more accepting over the years of the need for some of its members to use medication to treat co-occurring conditions. The following excerpts are from the pamphlet, *The AA Member—Medications & Other Drugs*, that was published in 1984.

> Because of the difficulties that many alcoholics have with drugs, some members have taken the position that no one in AA should take any medication. While this position has undoubtedly prevented relapses for some, it has meant disaster for others.
>
> It becomes clear that just as it is wrong to enable or support any alcoholic to become readdicted to any drug, it is equally wrong to deprive any alcoholic of medication which can alleviate or control other disabling physical and/or emotional problems.[8]

In spite of the opinions you may hear in 12-step meetings, Alcoholics Anonymous World Services, Inc., which writes AA approved literature, does not subscribe to the belief that alcoholics should abstain from medications to treat legitimate health concerns. The people with the "don't take anything" beliefs seem to be quieting down as they learn more about the many co-occurring conditions of addiction. Please don't let the opinions of others keep you from getting the help you deserve.

With a greater understanding of how these medications

work, and with more awareness of their low abuse potential when closely monitored, you will have the information you need to make your decision regarding medication. Other important information to consider is your stage of recovery.

STAGES OF RECOVERY

The stage of recovery you are in is important in your decision to take medication. I have adapted the following stages from the work of Gorski and Miller.[9]

Pretreatment
This is the phase before alcoholics or addicts enter treatment. The addiction is out of control. This is *not* the time to initiate treatment for AD/HD with medication. The priority of this stage is to move into addiction treatment.

Stabilization
This includes a period of physical and emotional detox. During this stage, alcoholics and addicts may experience withdrawal symptoms and can be quite ill. This is also *not* the time to treat AD/HD.

Early Recovery
For many, this is a time of great confusion and turmoil. You have made a commitment to recovery but may feel ambivalent. Early recovery is not an ideal time to treat AD/HD with medication unless AD/HD is clearly hindering your ability to participate in recovery programs.

I have worked with people who had a history of relapse and whose AD/HD greatly impacted their ability to get to treatment regularly, let alone focus enough to get much from 12-step meetings, after-care groups, or therapy. Their AD/HD impulsiveness also contributed to their inability to avoid taking that first drink, puff, hit, or line. For these people, treatment for AD/HD, including the use of medication, was helpful, if not essential. In each case, the individuals were extremely motivated and actively involved in a program of recovery. They worked closely with a psychiatrist who carefully monitored their medication. They also attended weekly therapy sessions and had the support of friends in recovery.

Treating AD/HD with medications during early recovery can prevent future relapse for some. The potential risk of giving medication to someone who is newly sober must be weighed carefully against the benefit. The key to successful treatment rests in a comprehensive treatment plan.

Middle Recovery

This is the time to create a life based on recovery. For many, this means huge emotional, spiritual, relationship, living, and work changes. Middle recovery is the time when you can clearly see the effects of AD/HD. Assessing and treating AD/HD at this time can better enable you to work through personal issues, stay sober, and increase the quality of your life.

Ongoing Recovery

For many this is a time when life really begins to come together. You feel comfortable with recovery and can feel serene even during stormy times.

On the other hand, this may be the stage when recovering alcoholics and addicts who have AD/HD are feeling more anger, frustration, self-loathing, shame, and confusion than ever because they're struggling with the same issues they've struggled with all their lives. They still impulsively quit jobs and relationships, can't concentrate, and are either too active or can't get started at all. Treatment with medication can be life-altering and aid in preventing relapse.

MEDICATIONS AND NEUROTRANSMITTERS

The information you're about to read is based on recent studies from physicians and scientists who are on the leading edge of adult AD/HD treatment. Because research on AD/HD is advancing so quickly, there will be new information and possibly new medications before you read this book. The following brief overview provides basic information about the different medications used to treat AD/HD. This is not meant to take the place of medical information provided by your physician.

Earlier we discussed neurotransmitters and how imbalances in these messenger chemicals are believed to contribute to AD/HD. Dopamine, one of these neurotransmitters, works to relieve symptoms of AD/HD in ways similar to how antidepressants like Prozac, Paxil, Zoloft, or Lexapro work to rebalance serotonin. This is the key to relieving symptoms of biological depression. Most of the medication used to treat AD/HD has focused on dopamine, but medicines that work primarily with norepinephrine and serotonin levels are also being used.

Treating conditions at the neurotransmitter level is still not an exact science. The type of AD/HD and any co-occurring conditions will help your physician choose the medication(s) best for you. There is some trial and error. It's not uncommon for a patient to try two or three different medications, at different dosage levels, to find what works best. Your doctor should also help you find the best time(s) of day to take your medicine. Taking medication in the afternoon or evening may keep one person up late at night, while another may find that taking stimulant medication prior to going to bed actually helps him or her sleep.

Several different types of medications are now used to treat AD/HD and co-occurring conditions. Generally they fall into the following categories:

- Stimulants
- Nonstimulants
- Mood Stabilizers
- Antidepressants

Over the years researchers and physicians have found that medication approved for one condition can be helpful in treating other conditions. The antidepressant Wellbutrin can relieve AD/HD symptoms for some individuals. Interestingly, certain medications designed to treat seizures are being used effectively to stabilize mood. So you'll see various categories of medications used to treat AD/HD.

TREATMENT WITH STIMULANTS

When the subject of taking stimulants to treat AD/HD comes up, some people ask the question, "Am I going to be taking speed?" The answer may be yes or no. If you and your physician choose to use Dexedrine or Adderall, you will be taking amphetamine medication. Ritalin and other methylphenidate compounds like Concerta are mild stimulants but are not amphetamines.

Here are some important differences between taking prescribed medication and street drugs.

- Stimulant medication is taken orally, at specific times, in dosages that do not create a "high" or euphoria.
- Due to the low dosage and lack of euphoria, most people do not develop a tolerance to stimulant medication.
- The dosage and quality of medication will not vary. Street drugs can be diluted or cut with baby powder, ephedrine, and who knows what.
- Street amphetamines produce a "high" as a result of much higher doses (several hundred times higher) and the route of administration (smoking, snorting, injecting).
- The intense euphoria produced by high doses of street amphetamines can cause cravings for more and quickly lead to addiction.
- Unlike street drugs, your intake of stimulant medication will be closely monitored by your doctor and other members of your support system.

THE
BOTTOM
LINE

Good Safety Record

Stimulant medications have been used for over fifty years to treat attention problems, obesity, and narcolepsy. These medications, when used properly, have a good safety record with few side effects. If you're taking stimulants to treat your AD/HD, you should not feel euphoric, high, or wired. Instead, you should notice an increased ability to concentrate, focus, organize, and control your impulses and activity level. Amongst those who have high activity levels, many report feeling calmer, less restless, and less anxious when taking stimulants. For those who have low activity level AD/HD, many report feeling a more normal energy level.

If you're getting high, euphoric, or manic as a result of your AD/HD medication, something is wrong. Your dosage or type of medication needs to be adjusted; you may need to stop taking it or you may have conditions other than AD/HD. Stimulant medication can sometimes increase manic behavior in those with bipolar disorder. Please consult with your doctor before you make any changes in your medication.

- You are not the one to prescribe or change your dosage of medication.
- If you take more medication than is prescribed, you are self-medicating.
- If you take less than what is prescribed, you are self-medicating.
- Call your doctor before you make changes in your medication.
- Remember, self-medicating has caused you misery in the past and can cause you the loss of your recovery or your life.

Rebound

Rebound is a problem that can occur when taking stimulant medication, especially the short-acting types. When the level of medication increases in the bloodstream, AD/HD symptoms are diminished. When the blood level of medication is decreasing, its effectiveness is wearing off and AD/HD symptoms begin returning. The problem with rebound is that when the effectiveness of the medication drops off quickly, not only do AD/HD symptoms return, people feel worse than they did prior to taking their meds.

Some of the symptoms of rebound are irritability, agitation, sleepiness, confusion, depressed mood, and generally feeling miserable. All of these symptoms are temporary. Rebound can be avoided by taking the next dose of medication before the last dose begins wearing off. Long lasting or extended released preparations help maintain consistent levels of medication, thus preventing rebound symptoms for most people. Changing the type of medication or adjusting the dose or time medication is taken can increase its effectiveness and decrease side effects.

Let's start our discussion of specific stimulant medications with the one that has the highest profile and is the most controversial.

Ritalin

Ritalin (methylphenidate) has proven to be effective in treating AD/HD. Contrary to popular belief, Ritalin is one of the most studied medications with a better safety record than most medications commonly prescribed. The use of Ritalin has increased due to better awareness, diagnosis, and treatment of AD/HD in adults and children. The increase in stimulant use can be compared to the increase in insulin use. Once insulin was found to be an effective treatment for diabetes, insulin use skyrocketed.

Ritalin is a mild central nervous system stimulant believed to increase the activity of dopamine, which relieves or diminishes AD/HD symptoms. The most common side effects (decreased appetite, sleep disturbances, stomachaches, headaches, and anxiety) are usually mild and manageable by changing the dose and time Ritalin is taken.

This is not to say that Ritalin is 100 percent safe and everyone with AD/HD should take it. There are potential risks when you take any medication; even aspirin can cause problems for some. As with any medication, it is important to weigh the potential risks and gains, and work closely with your doctor so that he or she can monitor your dosage to achieve the greatest level of effectiveness.

Pharmaceutical companies have been working hard to create time-released methylphenidate delivery systems. These medications include Metadate, Concerta, Focolin, Ritalin LA, and Ritalin-SR.

Concerta

Concerta is a commonly used methylphenidate compound with a unique delivery system. The capsule is coated with an immediate release dose. There are two chambers in the capsule. There is a push agent that releases the morning dose and also releases the afternoon dose. This makes for a smooth time-released delivery of the medication that lasts for eight to twelve hours depending on the individual.

Dexedrine

Dexedrine (dextroamphetamine) is an amphetamine stimulant that, milligram for milligram, is stronger than Ritalin and works a bit differently. We don't know exactly why, but some people respond better to one stimulant than to another. Dexedrine comes in tablets that work for approximately four hours, and time-released capsules called spansules, which work for six to eight hours. Rebound effects happen more often on the short acting Dexedrine than the longer acting spansules.

Adderall

Adderall (dextroamphetamine and amphetamine) is a mixture of four amphetamine salts that are absorbed and leave the blood-stream at different curves, which overlap in ways that provide a smooth onset and slow drop off. Adderall is available in tablets that last four to six hours and extended release capsules which last six to eight hours depending on the person. The longer-acting preparations have the least rebound effect, which may actually decrease their abuse potential.

NONSTIMULANT MEDICATION

Wellbutrin

Wellbutrin (buproprion) is believed to work primarily with the neurotransmitters dopamine and norepinephrine, and has little impact on serotonin. It works very well for some, while others also need a stimulant medication. Wellbutrin is considered to have no abuse potential and is a good choice for people in recovery or those who have abused street amphetamines.

Strattera

Strattera (atomoxetine HCL), released in 2003, works primarily with the neurotransmitter norepinephrine. Like other medications used to treat AD/HD, Strattera works very well for some and not so well for others. It is considered to have no potential for abuse and may be a good choice for those in early recovery and those who have abused street amphetamines.

Provigil

Provigil (modafamil), initially used to treat narcolepsy, is used alone or in conjunction with stimulant medication. Provigil appears to be more helpful for keeping people alert than treating other symptoms such as impulsiveness, focus, and hyperactivity.

MOOD STABILIZERS

Mood management is an issue for many with AD/HD. Thomas E. Brown, PhD, who created the Brown AD/HD Assessment Evaluation, has a specific category for evaluating mood as part of the AD/HD picture. Some people suffer from a depressed mood, others from fluctuating moods that may be high or low as in bipolar disorders. Medications that were initially used to treat seizures can also help stabilize mood. Here are some medications your doctor may consider to help manage mood fluctuations:

- Trileptal
- Depakote
- Lamictal
- Lithium
- Neurontin

ANTIDEPRESSANT MEDICATIONS

The longer antidepressant medications are used, the more we realize how effective they are in treating conditions other than depression. Antidepressant medications that work only with serotonin seem to help some people with AD/HD by improving their ability to control their impulses and feel calmer. They do not, however, seem to improve attention for most people.

It is common practice among physicians to prescribe other medication along with a stimulant medication to treat AD/HD and co-occurring conditions. The following is a list of some of the nonstimulant medications used to treat different aspects of AD/HD and its many co-occurring conditions.

- Prozac
- Paxil
- Zoloft
- Clonidine
- Nortriptyline
- Wellbutrin
- Effexor
- Neurontin
- Lexapro
- Tenex
- Lamictal

IS STIMULANT MEDICATION RIGHT FOR YOU?

If you have a history of abusing street amphetamines or prescribed amphetamine diet pills, you may not be a good candidate for treatment with stimulant medication. Again, this is not an all-or-nothing proposition.

People with recent or ongoing histories of amphetamine abuse should consider nonstimulant medications such as Wellbutrin or Strattera. These medications can be effective and have little abuse potential. Some meth addicts with years of solid recovery can successfully take stimulants with close monitoring. However, their bodies can build a tolerance to the medication. The dose that provided symptom relief loses its effectiveness. One way physicians deal with this is by switching the patient to another stimulant when he or she reports that the dose isn't working as well. For example, the recovering addict may be on Ritalin; the body builds a tolerance; the doctor switches to Adderall. When the Adderall is less effective, the doctor may prescribe Dexedrine. By the time the person returns to Ritalin, it will take time for the body to build tolerance.

On the other hand, some who have abused street amphetamines do not build a tolerance, nor do they abuse non-amphetamine stimulant medication such as Ritalin or other methylphenidate compounds.

Stimulant Abuse and Addiction

There has been a flurry of media about the abuse of stimulant medications. Many news articles and television programs focus on young people abusing Ritalin, Adderall, and Dexedrine. The truth is, these medications can be abused and the abuser can become addicted. Unfortunately the media tends to draw erroneous conclusions, such as "The use of stimulant medication to treat AD/HD causes drug addiction." Research previously mentioned in this chapter states the opposite.

Most cases of stimulant abuse are among addicts who are not being treated for AD/HD. These are people who will abuse almost any drug if given the chance. Adderall and Dexadrine are abused by people who are trying to get effects similar to speed, such as feeling high, staying awake, cramming for finals, or to lose weight. Ritalin, however, is often abused as a last resort because it doesn't give users the euphoria they crave.

Some drug addicts and alcoholics abused stimulant medication by taking more than prescribed, or by grinding it up to inhale or to mix with water and inject. Some people learned how to present as though they had AD/HD in order to obtain stimulants. In most cases, these people had been given large prescriptions with little or no ongoing treatment for AD/HD or addiction. These are rare exceptions, and Carla is one of them.

From Diet Pills to Addiction

Carla was diagnosed with AD/HD in her late fifties. She had twenty plus years of sobriety. She was hesitant to take amphetamine medication because she was active in AA. Carla responded well to the medication. It reminded her of the two years she took benzadrine for weight loss. "I felt great, my home and life were well organized, and I got a lot done. My doctor took me off them because I didn't lose weight."

It took several years before Carla began abusing her medication. She would increase her dose when she wanted to get more accomplished. As she took much higher doses, she felt high and euphoric. Soon she was taking her entire month's supply of medication in one week. Carla would then tough it out until she could get a refill and repeat the cycle. "I knew I was addicted. My guilt and shame kept me away from AA meetings. I didn't want anyone to know my secret."

Eventually, Carla felt as though she was being eaten alive by her feelings of guilt and shame. She told her therapist and her doctor that she'd been abusing her medication. She went back to her friends at AA and told them the truth. Carla felt liberated from her addiction. Today Carla takes a nonstimulant medication to treat her AD/HD. Fortunately, she stopped her addiction to amphetamines and did not go back to her primary addiction to alcohol.

Of the hundreds of people I have worked with over the past fourteen years, I only know of five with histories of addiction who have abused their stimulant medication.

WILL I BE ON MEDICATION FOREVER?

It depends on how you want or need to function.

Everyone responds to medication differently, depending on the type of medication, the severity of AD/HD, and activities of daily life. Some people take medication for the better part of their lives because the consequences are so severe when they stop. Their AD/HD medication may contribute to keeping them clean and sober, employed, in relationships, and out of prison. Others find that after months or years on medication, they are able to change troublesome behavior. The medication assists their brain in learning new ways to adapt to their AD/HD behavior. This is especially true for those whose AD/HD symptoms have not had a severe impact on their daily living. Some of these individuals are able to go off their medication.

Some individuals with AD/HD have functioned their entire lives without medication and can continue to function without it. What they find, however, is that instead of struggling to get through each day, medication helps them thrive in ways they never thought were possible. Taking medication significantly improves the quality of their lives and the lives of those around them. After functioning with a brain that works with them rather than against them, they usually don't choose to go back to their former AD/HD state.

People may choose to go off medication when they experience major life changes that don't require them to function at previous levels. This may be true if their children leave home, if they retire, if they move to a place where it's quieter and less overwhelming, or if they find a job that requires less focused attention and more divergent thinking and high energy levels.

GETTING THE RIGHT MEDICATION

Once you've found a doctor you feel comfortable with, tell him or her if you self-medicated your AD/HD. Be prepared to volunteer your complete history of substance use and addiction, even if your physician doesn't ask. The doctor may not realize how important this information is. You may be the one to help educate your doctor about AD/HD and addictions. Many resourceful people with AD/HD have contributed to the higher education of medical professionals.

When taking prescribed medication, especially during the first month or so, it's important to have phone contact and/or a frequent appointment with your doctor. You can create a simple chart with numbers ranging from one to ten. With this chart you can graph your mood, concentration, energy level, and impulse control. This gives you and your doctor important information about how your medication is working.

Depending on the effectiveness or any side effects, your doctor may want to alter the dosage and perhaps the type of medication you're taking. This is a fairly common practice. The important thing is that you're getting the best results with the least number of side effects. Taking your medication with food or changing the dosage or time you take it usually remedies side effects such as difficulty sleeping, anxiety, or stomach upset.

A note of caution: Chocolate and caffeinated drinks (such as tea, cola, and coffee) may cause you to feel anxious and shaky if you combine them with stimulant medication. When people decrease or eliminate caffeine, they find that the anxiety and nervousness also decrease.

"I Won't Take Drugs, No Matter What"

Roberto learned that smoking hashish (a potent form of marijuana) and shooting heroin helped him survive and tolerate the daily fear, anxiety, and boredom he experienced while serving in Vietnam. Roberto was able to stop his heroin use when he returned home, but he was dependent on smoking pot to get through the day and sleep at night.

Thirty years later, this fifty-five-year-old man came to see me because, "I can't smoke one more bowl or joint. My lungs hurt, I cough all the time, my memory is shot, my wife is sick of me, I hate myself . . . and I can't stop."

Roberto was committed to stopping and staying stopped. He experienced physical and emotional withdrawal symptoms. He felt irritable, anxious, and agitated. He couldn't eat much and didn't sleep well for several weeks. Roberto said, "I can deal with the physical stuff, but the constant craving, the thoughts about smoking, are driving me crazy." But he didn't smoke and gradually began feeling better. He joined a veterans recovery group and continued with weekly therapy. Roberto had been clean for eight months when I began to see that some of his difficulties were no longer marijuana-related, but were related to AD/HD.

It wasn't difficult for Roberto to accept his diagnosis of AD/HD, because his brother and niece had it. It was, however, difficult for him to accept that medication could help improve the quality of his life. "I'm not taking drugs, no matter what." Roberto went on to say what many long-term marijuana smokers say, "Pot is natural. It comes from the earth. I'm not taking drugs—they can have bad side effects, you never know what they can do to you."

Roberto and I periodically clashed on the idea of him even considering an evaluation for medication. I took a different approach and asked Roberto if he would be willing to have his brother Jorge come in and talk about his experience taking medication. Roberto agreed, probably in hopes that I would stop bugging him.

Jorge told his older brother how taking medication for his AD/HD had changed his life. He also shared how well his daughter Cynthia was doing in school since she'd been on medication.

Jorge was able to do for Roberto what I could not. By sharing his experience as family, Roberto became willing to try medication.

As of this writing Roberto has been clean and sober for five years. He comes in for a "tune up" about twice a year. He shares how much his life has improved with the help of his medication. We're both able to chuckle about the man who "wouldn't take drugs, no matter what."

Now that you have a better understanding of the role of medication and some tools to change your behavior, it's important to appreciate the potential for relapse. The next chapter provides you with practical ways to prevent AD/HD and addiction relapses.

GETTING BETTER, STAYING BETTER

preventing
AD/HD
and
addiction
relapses

ARE YOU FINISHED, DONE with it, tired of quitting only to start again? Or are you someone in recovery who wants to stay there? Do you want to understand how your AD/HD contributes to you ending up in bed with a box of donuts, a pipe full of pot, or a bottle of Jack Daniels, even after you thought you'd quit? Are you ready to step off the merry-go-round, plant your feet firmly in recovery, and stop the spinning of addiction for good and for all?

Anyone can stop an addiction for the moment. But can you stay stopped? How many times have you said, "After I finish this cake, I'll never eat another piece." "I promise I will never drink and drive again," or "God, if you get me out of this, I will never gamble again." When you promised to stop, you absolutely meant it. You were dead serious and desperate to stop your addiction. You tried your hardest, but before you knew it, you found yourself doing the same old thing again. Your best efforts failed.

You are not alone. Millions of people stop their substance abuse or addictive behavior every day, only to fall back into it within days or months. Stopping isn't the issue. Staying stopped is. You may have tried to control or change your behavior by yourself, or you may have sought professional help. Maybe you've been involved in a 12-step recovery program or you are right now. If you've given quitting your best shot but are having trouble maintaining abstinence, there may be underlying issues that are preventing you from attaining and maintaining your recovery.

You may have an understanding of how the term relapse applies to addiction recovery but wonder how one can have an AD/HD relapse. We'll take a look at how the process of relapse affects AD/HD and addiction recovery, and you will learn strategies to prevent this painful and life-threatening process. But first we need to understand exactly what a relapse is.

WHAT IS A RELAPSE?

Relapse is a term used to describe returning to a former condition. Relapse doesn't always mean that a person returns to drug, food, or alcohol use. People with other medical illnesses have relapses when their conditions return to where they were after having a period of improvement or partial recovery.

Terence T. Gorski and Merlene Miller pioneered this concept in their groundbreaking book, *Counseling for Relapse Prevention* (1982). Gorski and Miller minimized the moral judgments regarding relapse by describing the physical, emotional, and behavioral aspects of this process.[1]

When we understand that having a relapse means returning to a former state of being, we can use this model when discussing AD/HD recovery as well. AD/HD and addictions are never cured, but there are many things you can do to maintain the improvements you make. Knowing what you can do to help yourself when you slide back into old thinking and behaviors is essential. You don't have to live with old behaviors and addictions that are harmful.

Relapse Is a Process, Not an Event

Relapse isn't an instantaneous event. Relapse, for most people, happens over time. Look at The Addiction Relapse Continuum that follows; it may help clarify what I'm about to say. Recovery and relapse are mutually exclusive states; in other words, when you're in recovery, you're not in relapse. You can't do both at the same time, just like you can't drink and at the same time be abstinent.

Relapse is a temporary state, and it can end in two ways. One is by returning completely, and perhaps permanently, to the behaviors, substances, or illness you were recovering from. The other is by returning to your recovery. First let's look at addiction relapse and suggestions for continued recovery, then do the same for AD/HD recovery.

THE ADDICTION RELAPSE CONTINUUM

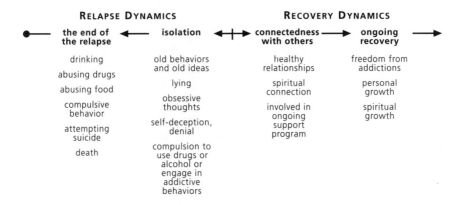

RELAPSE DYNAMICS		RECOVERY DYNAMICS	
the end of the relapse	isolation	connectedness with others	ongoing recovery
drinking	old behaviors and old ideas	healthy relationships	freedom from addictions
abusing drugs	lying	spiritual connection	personal growth
abusing food	obsessive thoughts	involved in ongoing support program	spiritual growth
compulsive behavior	self-deception, denial		
attempting suicide	compulsion to use drugs or alcohol or engage in addictive behaviors		
death			

You may want to take a moment and locate your position on the continuum. Be honest with yourself. Are you on the recovery or relapse side of the line? As you can see by the continuum, you may be in the process of relapse and not have taken a drink or a drug. Relapse is crossing over the imaginary line of recovery and returning to your old ideas and behaviors. Your denial may tell you that you're not really addicted. Your alcoholism may tell you that you can drink socially, even though you've always lost control when you drink.

If you find yourself on the relapse side of the line, you may be feeling isolated from others. Maybe you've stopped participating in your recovery program. You may find that your thinking has returned to old territory. You may have convinced yourself that you can eat sugar, even though you have a proven track record that you can't. You may also engage in dishonest behavior, experience rage attacks, and feel ill at ease.

If not treated, your relapse will progress. If you don't get help to cross back into recovery, you risk feeling guilty, ashamed, isolated, depressed, confused, resentful, and all the other painful feelings you used substances and behaviors to avoid.

The last step of a relapse is to punish yourself. You begin to seek relief in substances and behaviors that will hurt you and ultimately make you feel even worse about yourself. Many people have no idea they are in the process of relapse. They find themselves drinking, smoking pot, gambling, or binge eating, and have no idea what happened. You don't have to do this to yourself. If you're over the line, now is the time to get the support you deserve.

Living on the recovering side of the continuum means you feel connected with others—to family, friends, and community. You are growing emotionally and spiritually and living a clean and sober life. You feel a sense of belonging. You feel your pain without looking to drugs and old behaviors to soothe or mask it. You are developing a group of friends who enjoy their lives without participating in addictions. You practice principles of recovery in your daily living. Actively being in recovery does not mean that your life will always be smooth as glass or that you will never have adversities. Life happens, in and out of recovery. The good news is that in recovery you have better judgment and ability to handle life's challenges.

It's common for people in recovery to have times when they hover near the dividing line between recovery and relapse. No matter how hard you work in your recovery program, how many 12-step meetings, therapy sessions, and support groups you attend, there will be times when you cross into relapse territory. This happens to people with many years of recovery, but it doesn't mean you have to take the relapse subway to the end of the line. You can switch directions as soon as you realize you're heading for a destination you don't want to go to.

Why People Relapse into Addictions

People relapse primarily because they are undertreated. People don't relapse because they are bad or don't care. They relapse because they are not getting enough treatment for their addictions. They also relapse because other co-occurring conditions are not being treated properly. Most people who overindulge or have dependency issues have a variety of complex challenges to work through. If these issues are not treated in a comprehensive way, it will be difficult to maintain abstinence from addictive substances and behaviors.

How AD/HD Contributes to Relapse

Treatment programs used to focus primarily on helping people stay sober and work through issues directly related to their drinking or drug use. Today, as knowledge of what is called "dual diagnosis" or what I refer to as "multiple diagnosis" is growing, some treatment programs also treat mood disorders, anxiety disorders, eating disorders, and family-related problems.

Unfortunately, not all addiction and eating disorder specialists assess or treat AD/HD. If you seek treatment, make sure the health-care professional or treatment program treats AD/HD. There is also fear among many chemical dependency treatment providers regarding the treatment of "emotional" problems with medication. What is often misunderstood is that many of these "emotional" problems have a medical or biological basis that must be treated as well. Treating AD/HD may be a large part of completing the puzzle of recovery for many people. If AD/HD is not treated, the puzzle has a huge hole in it. Untreated AD/HD may be keeping people from a life of recovery, fulfillment, and serenity that is beyond their wildest dreams.

Sometimes people in recovery report being "struck drunk." They find themselves drinking in a bar or at a party without realizing what they're doing until it's too late. In most cases, however, those who return from a relapse can describe the sequence of events and the changes in attitudes and thinking that preceded their use of drugs, alcohol, or addictive behaviors. With help, and the aid of 20/20 hindsight, many individuals are able to gain understanding into the process that led them back to their addictions.

Some will describe feeling so good in their sober life that they drifted away from what was supporting their recovery. Others report convincing themselves that they could smoke pot on occasion and, before they knew it, they were smoking daily again. For others, their relapse was preceded by an event, a crisis, the upsurge of painful memories, the death of a loved one, or resentments they could not get over.

Untreated AD/HD may be making it even harder for you to remain abstinent from drugs, alcohol, or other addictions. While relapse is a process, for people with AD/HD that process can be an extremely short one. People with untreated AD/HD have a greater risk of relapsing due to a difficulty or inability to control their impulses. These people often truly feel they were struck drunk. They may be totally unaware of their relapse signals and impulsively return to substances, food, and behavioral addictions. For many the relapse process can take days, months, or even years; for some people with AD/HD impulsiveness, the process can happen in the blink of an eye.

THREE KINDS OF ADDICTION RELAPSE

The Nontherapeutic Relapse

A nontherapeutic relapse occurs when people slip back into addictions and either never return to recovery, or return with no understanding about why they relapsed or how they will prevent another relapse in the future. They often deny the seriousness of their addictions during and after relapse. Even if they are fortunate enough to get back to recovery, they are at high risk of relapsing in the future. Not even the pain of their relapse or its consequences are enough to help them change their attitude, thinking, or behavior.

The nontherapeutic relapse is common among people with AD/HD because they may not truly understand the concept of cause and effect. It is hard for them to think through the consequences of a relapse and thus take the steps to prevent it. I work with individuals who are on probation or parole and who intellectually understand the consequences of drinking or using drugs again. They've told me they never want to be locked up again. Yet they run into an old friend and within minutes they're drinking, taking drugs, and sometimes, committing impulsive crimes.

Many alcoholics and addicts do not have the chance to return to treatment after a relapse. Some live hopelessly stuck in their addictions, while others are institutionalized. And many die. It's tragic that they lose their lives, and the tragedy is compounded because their plight is misunderstood. They are regarded by some as stupid, bad, or professional criminals with no sense of right or wrong. Their families and loved ones suffer feelings of guilt, shame, and powerlessness because they were unable to change the course of events.

The Therapeutic Relapse

A therapeutic relapse occurs when alcoholics, addicts, and those with eating disorders are able to return to recovery and gain valuable insight regarding their relationship with food, drugs, alcohol, or addictive behaviors. A therapeutic relapse removes doubts about whether or not they can ever drink or use drugs without consequences. They are more accepting that their addictions make them feel worse rather than better.

With a therapeutic relapse comes surrender to the fact that old ideas and ways of living are harmful and potentially deadly. After a therapeutic relapse, the individual is more able to accept help from others. With a therapeutic relapse comes a stronger commitment to recovery and to life.

Suicide, the Ultimate Relapse

For some people, untreated physical, emotional, and spiritual pain, and self-loathing become so intense that suicide feels like the only way to relieve the suffering. Some people take their lives by relapsing and accidentally or intentionally killing themselves with their addictions. Others make a decision to take their lives without returning to their addictions. These people are usually suffering from untreated or undertreated problems such as mood disorders, shame, AD/HD, PTSD, anxiety disorders, and schizophrenia.

The risk of a successful suicide attempt is greater when mind-altering substances are used. Drugs and alcohol can inhibit your judgment and increase impulsiveness. Untreated AD/HD can also increase the risk of suicidal thoughts becoming a reality, because AD/HD hampers impulse control in ways similar to drugs and alcohol. At highest risk are the people with AD/HD who use substances. They can completely lose control of their impulses and end up dead, even if they did not really want to die.

Suicidal thinking in sobriety indicates that you are not receiving adequate treatment for all your problems. If you feel that your only choices are returning to your addictions or committing suicide, something is wrong. Help is available. Talk to someone immediately about your thoughts of suicide and seek professional help.

ABSTAINING AND MISERABLE

You may be one of the fortunate ones who is actively recovering from dependency on substances and behaviors. Congratulations! You have a lot of courage and are on a path that will save your life. But what if the life you're trying to save feels worse than the drunken, stoned, overindulging life you lived? Did you think all your problems would vanish when you gave up your addiction? Did you fantasize about the perfect life you would live if only you could get sober? How disillusioning to wake up sober and feel overwhelmed by the wreckage of your life. How discouraging to feel that daily life is still harder for you than those around you. How despairing to be in recovery, feel worse, and know that food, alcohol, and drugs are no longer an option to relieve your pain. There is hope.

You Are Not Alone

Almost everyone who lets go of self-medicating feels worse for a time. Simply stopping addictive behavior will not treat the issues you've been attempting to deal with by drinking, using drugs, or acting in compulsive ways. Now you get to work through the underlying emotional and sometimes mental conditions that have been with you all along. Now you get to work through the trauma you most likely experienced throughout your life. Now you have the opportunity to learn to live life on life's terms. And now you don't get to medicate your pain with food, alcohol, or street drugs.

No wonder people relapse. Early recovery often doesn't feel good. It can be a time of great emotional pain, soul searching, grief, and, paradoxically, tremendous joy and gratitude. Some people enter recovery and float on what is referred to as a "pink cloud." They feel wonderful to be released from the bondage of addictions. Over time, though, many will fall through the pink cloud of early bliss and hit the reality of life.

Some people in recovery continue to feel miserable, even after months or years of hard work and commitment. Not only are their lives unmanageable, they feel guilty, ashamed, frustrated, and desperate, because even with years of recovery and therapy their lives are still chaotic. After too many years of miserable sobriety, some look for the comfort they believe drugs, food, and alcohol will provide. Once they return to their addictions, their lives really crumble. Some make it back to try again, but too many end up incarcerated or dead.

CAN AD/HD MEDICATION CAUSE ADDICTION RELAPSE?

Absolutely! Does this happen frequently? Absolutely not!

Can *untreated AD/HD* cause addiction relapse? Absolutely! This is a very important point, and one that people recovering from alcoholism and drug addiction need to understand. Even though we talked about medication in chapter 14, it deserves further discussion. If you have any concerns about taking stimulant medication, talk with your doctor about taking a nonstimulant medication. There are four important questions to answer before you consider taking stimulant medication to treat your AD/HD:

- How strong is your commitment to maintaining your recovery and treating your AD/HD?
- How closely will your medication be monitored?
- Do you have a comprehensive treatment plan that addresses your AD/HD and addictions, as well as other co-occurring conditions?
- Do you participate in 12-step programs and recovery groups, and have a support system of recovering people in your life?

I see recovering addicts who have had years of psychotherapy and treatment for conditions other than AD/HD. Some are on the verge of suicide or relapse; others are depressed and feel vanquished. They are exhausted, spent, burned out, and tired of trying to live sober with a disability they may not even know they have. They deserve more from their recovery. They don't have to suffer from untreated AD/HD or become readdicted. They can have both problems treated.

For those who make it into ongoing recovery, their response to AD/HD treatment is usually quite remarkable and they are not at high risk to abuse stimulant medication unless they're already in the process of relapse. The problem isn't that they want medication; the problem is more likely that they don't want to take medication. Many deny themselves treatment for fear they will jeopardize their sobriety.

RELAPSE PREVENTION

The best way to prevent a relapse is to make sure that all of your conditions are being properly treated. Your willingness to be honest with yourself, your health-care providers, and people in your support network is essential. Feel free to refer to the previous chapter for the details of a comprehensive treatment program. Covering all of your bases is your best bet. Let's start by briefly looking at medication again.

Medication
Research statistics regarding treatment with stimulant medications for AD/HD and relapse are not abundant because the field is new. However, experts who have treated adults with AD/HD and addictions believe in the efficacy of medication: "Studies by Wender and coworkers (1995) and Satel and Nelson, among

others, demonstrate that most patients do not develop tolerance to, nor become dependent on, stimulant drugs."[2]

Most people in recovery respond to stimulant medication by feeling more in control of their thoughts and behavior, including those that can lead to relapse. They are able to concentrate and follow through with goals and tasks, which in turn increases their self-esteem. Many report feeling more alert, present, and aware of their feelings. Once recovering people experience the benefit of their medication, most do not want to even consider abusing it, because they enjoy feeling "normal."

HOW DO I KNOW IF I'M ABUSING MY MEDICATION?

You shouldn't consider taking medication unless you are clear about the following:

- Your sole motive is to improve your AD/HD symptoms.
- You are committed to being rigorously honest with your doctor, therapist, family members, and recovery support group or sponsor.
- You will only take medication as prescribed.
- You will not alter your dosage without your doctor's permission.
- You will never give or sell your medication to others.
- If you feel high or wired on your medication, you will call your doctor immediately.
- You will not take medication to increase productivity, pull all-nighters, or function in superhuman ways.

If you are able to commit to the above, you know you will be using your medication correctly.

I Want More

Most people who overindulge or become addicted want more. For some of us, "more" was the first word we uttered. Your addictive thinking may say, "If it tastes good, or feels good, why not have more?" You know why having more is not the answer—because you reach the place where even too much is not enough.

It makes absolute sense that if you find something that gives you better concentration, focused energy, and greater productivity, you will want more. This can be a slippery place. There is a subtle line you can cross over. One side of the line is using your medication to improve your AD/HD symptoms. The other is using your medication to increase your productivity in ways that become harmful to you.

You can abuse your medication when you use it to hyperfocus on work or activities to the point that your health and relationships suffer. Even though your intentions are not to get high or loaded, you are abusing your medication if it enables you to lock into focusing on only a few things. When this hyperfocusing disrupts other areas of your life, and you can't stop doing it, you have a problem. Sound familiar?

This doesn't mean you have to stop your medication. You may need your dosage adjusted so that your attention doesn't get stuck and is able to shift freely. You may need help modulating your energy throughout different aspects of your life. AD/HD medication is not meant to make you superhuman.

Abusing AD/HD Medication

If you are an alcoholic or addict, you may at some time think about abusing your medication. If you are properly medicated, your AD/HD symptoms will be decreased, yet you will not feel high or euphoric. The sleeping "addict" part of your brain will wake up from time to time and want to be fed. Even after years of recovery, your brain can give you a ton of good reasons why you should go to Vegas, or put substances in your body from which you have abstained.

You don't have to follow through with these self-destructive obsessions that sound like such a good idea at the time. This is why ongoing recovery is so important. Besides, many people who take more of their medication than is prescribed often feel ashamed, shaky, nervous, and guilty.

Here are some suggestions on handling the temptation to abuse your medication:

- Admit to yourself that you're thinking of experimenting or getting high on your AD/HD medication.
- Tell someone immediately. Call your doctor, therapist, sponsor, friend (who understands your addiction), or another person in recovery.
- Tell the truth about what you are thinking or what you have done.

- Try not to let your shame keep you from getting help now. It's not too late.
- Let your doctor, therapist, and support team help you create plans to prevent future relapses.
- If you continue to abuse your medication, your doctor may need to switch you to other medication.

Some addicts and alcoholics cannot use stimulant medication safely. If you are one of these, you are not bad—you are an addict. There are other medications your doctor can prescribe that have little addiction potential.

Most people in recovery do not have problems with AD/HD medications. If you have problems taking only the prescribed amount, it isn't necessarily because you are self-destructive. It may just mean that you need more structure, supervision, and treatment for your addictions.

AD/HD RELAPSE

You may be wondering, "How can I relapse into AD/HD?" Because relapse is a return to a previous state, you can have an AD/HD relapse in a variety of ways. One thing that can happen is that your AD/HD symptoms get worse. This can happen for a variety of reasons. Stress levels may have increased in your life. You may not be aware that you have forgotten to take your medication. Some professionals believe that AD/HD medication has a high potential for abuse. If this were true, why do so many with AD/HD forget to take it? Those with AD/HD who are addicted to sugar, alcohol, or street drugs sure don't forget to use them.

Remembering to take medication at the prescribed times is a major challenge for many with AD/HD. If you forget to take your medicine or take it periodically, you are in AD/HD relapse. Create systems to remind yourself and ask those in your life for help.

Relapse dynamics also happen when you're not getting enough help and support. As with addictions, you may feel isolated, intolerant of yourself, and ashamed, and fall into old thinking and behavior. AD/HD relapse thinking occurs when you go into denial about AD/HD being a neurological difference and start believing that you're just stupid and lazy. You may even doubt you really have AD/HD, or wonder if AD/HD isn't just another fad the drug companies cooked up to make money. Before you know it, you've convinced yourself that you don't have AD/HD, that you are a rotten human being, and that you're unworthy of treatment and support. You may find yourself back in the grips of your out-of-control AD/HD symptoms.

Similar to the addiction relapse, the AD/HD relapse can be a process that ends in two ways. One is that you move yourself to the recovery side of the continuum by getting help and support. The other is that your life gets so painful and chaotic that you either return to addictions, lose your ability to function, or become incarcerated or institutionalized. In some cases, AD/HD relapse ends in suicide.

It is essential to have someone in your life whom you trust to give honest feedback if you're moving down the AD/HD relapse continuum. Remember, denial can be powerful. It may take a tremendous amount of energy to stay grounded in reality. If you have AD/HD, the reality is that you will feel better, function better, get along better with others, and be a more productive member of your community when your AD/HD is treated.

Ongoing Treatment for AD/HD

While therapy that focuses on AD/HD can be highly valuable, traditional therapy alone is usually not effective in treating AD/HD. You may find that a relationship with an AD/HD coach is helpful for a short period of time, or you may incorporate an AD/HD coach into your ongoing recovery program. The amount of support you need depends on the severity of your AD/HD and how you need to function in your life. The important thing is not to forget that your brain works differently from those who don't have AD/HD, and this difference can be disabling. Your AD/HD differences can become great assets if you are properly treated.

Ongoing treatment for your AD/HD can include the following:

- Working with a therapist who has expertise treating AD/HD
- Taking prescribed medication when indicated (and taking it as prescribed)
- Talking with others who understand AD/HD
- Joining an ongoing AD/HD support group
- Participating in online chat rooms with others who have AD/HD
- Attending AD/HD conferences

- Joining organizations such as the Attention Deficit Disorder Association (ADDA) (www.add.org)
- Attending Children & Adults with Attention Deficit Disorders (CHADD) groups (www.chadd.org)
- Working with an AD/HD coach
- Subscribing to magazines such as ADDitude, which has articles on children and adults, and ADDvance, which is geared toward women and girls

Don't Throw the Baby out with the Bath Water

AD/HD and addictions do not usually travel alone; they are often accompanied by a variety of co-occurring conditions. It's important to get help for everything that is hindering your ability to work, love, and enjoy life.

It's time to let go of the stigma and shame associated with AD/HD, addictions, and relapse. Unfortunately, we live in a society that is quick to make negative judgments about human conditions. The first step in changing these cultural attitudes is to change your own beliefs. You will continue to perpetuate unrealistic standards, misinformation, and prejudices until you are able to accept your own humanness. When you accept your AD/HD, addictions, and any other co-occurring problems, you begin to let go of your judgments about yourself. By accepting who you are, you are better able to accept others as they are. And so it goes.

IT'S NOT OVER YET

CONGRATULATIONS FOR GETTING TO the end of this book. If you read like I do, you may have started here to see if the rest of the book is worth reading. Or you may have skipped here to find "the solutions." It doesn't matter. The important thing is that you have arrived. You are at a place you've never been before. And that's what making changes is all about. You're taking a risk to enter uncharted waters. Some of you may have no problems entering uncharted waters, climbing mountains, hang gliding, or bungee jumping. For some with AD/HD this type of thrill-seeking risk is actually more comfortable than taking emotional risks. It's much more difficult to look at how you use food, drugs, alcohol, and behaviors to cover up or soothe inner pain.

Where Do I Go from Here?

The ending of this book is the beginning of a new phase of work. Continue the work you are doing if it's working for you. You may now realize that you have a lot of work in front of you. Don't worry—you have plenty of time to do it. Assess your needs and be willing to get help. This may mean doing some things that are not comfortable, like telling the truth to yourself and others. It may also mean joining therapy or 12-step groups. Remember you don't have to do it alone. Please don't let your pride or shame keep you from getting the help you deserve.

I hope you have found resources in this book to help you

with your specific problems. But all the resources, insight, and self-knowledge won't help unless you get yourself into action. Now is the time to reach out to others. This is hard for many of us with AD/HD, but you may not have other options, unless you're willing to continue living the way you are. By the way, if you have an eating disorder or addiction, it will only get worse without treatment. And that's a guarantee.

No More Secrets

We all have secrets, things we don't want anyone to know. You may fear that if others know your secrets, they won't love you anymore. This is the farthest from the truth. Those who love you will feel even closer to you as you are able to share your secrets. A wise saying goes like this, "The secret is, to have no secrets." This doesn't mean rush out and tell the world that you are a sex addict or bulimic. Be cautious. Pick carefully those you choose to share with. If you share too much with too many, you risk overexposing yourself and feeling ashamed. Watch out for AD/HD impulsivity, combined with the desire to get "well" right now.

This is where a good therapist comes in. Someone you can tell everything to, all of it. And know that it will never leave the room. A good therapist will guide you as you decide what and how you want to share with those you love.

What Is a Good Therapist?

A good therapist is first and foremost a good person. By that I mean a person with compassion, empathy, and true care and concern for you, the client or patient. Someone who is more than just his or her credential. Someone who is able to be present and real with you while maintaining professional boundaries. Therapists who have had to fight their own demons and stand up to their personal challenges have more to offer than academic solutions or active listening. The best therapists I know have therapists of their own. Being in therapy helps therapists stay clear about their issues and not confuse them with yours. Good therapists don't have to be in therapy now, yet they should have spent years in therapy working on their issues. I've learned so much about therapy by being in therapy myself. You see, the more therapists learn about themselves and deal with their issues, the better they can serve you. A therapist can't take you any further than he or she has gone.

Therapy is a well-defined partnership. It's a journey that two people embark on. The therapist is your guide, and the journey is yours. The details of the therapeutic relationship are well laid out in writing. Before you enter therapy you should know what fee you will be charged, how long sessions last, and how often you will meet. For more information refer to chapter 7 on getting the right diagnosis.

You don't have to settle with feeling miserable. It's even harder to continue to abuse yourself when you know you don't have to. Take what works for you from this book. Try some of the suggestions, even if they are scary. Nothing is more frightening than drinking, drugging, eating, or starving yourself to death.

Smashing the Stigmas

A stigma is a negative judgment of someone or a group of some-ones. A stigma is a mark of shame or discredit. Stigma results from ignorance, stereotyping, or a refusal to take in new information. Stigmas are also a result of fear—the fear of getting close to people who are different from us. If we get close to people who are different, we might just see how similar we really are.

If you feel judged or stigmatized by your AD/HD, eating dis-orders, or addictions, remember that others might be making you "wrong" so that they don't have to face their own issues. As long as they convince themselves you have brought your problems upon yourself, they don't have to feel their own vul-nerability. Their judgments are defenses against feeling their own shame.

It takes guts and courage to be yourself. Being you may not be easy. A teenager sat in my office while his parents complained about how hard it was living with him. I almost cried as he said to his parents with tears rolling down his cheeks, "If you think it's hard living with me, try being me."

Healing

Healing is the act of being restored to a state of health. For some, being restored to a state of health means healing wounds that are old and deep. These wounds may be inflamed and infected. It takes time—healing doesn't occur immediately. The amount and type of injury will determine your course of healing. You have a role in your healing. Your willingness to go to any lengths to heal makes a tremendous difference. Part of healing is sharing your experiences with others. Sharing your feelings of anger and agony, confusion and concerns, frustrations and fears, health and hope. Sharing your victories and triumphs no matter how small or how great.

Healing is accepting yourself as you are at this very moment, with all your flaws, bumps, and warts. Healing is letting go of your illusions and delusions of who you think you should be, how you think you should look, how you think you should act. It is accepting your AD/HD and other conditions, however they express themselves in your life. You can't get help until you accept you have problems.

Shame makes it hard to accept all of who we are. Healing is staying committed to getting the help you deserve for all of your issues. Healing is accepting that it takes a lifetime to change and grow. And this is your lifetime, no one else's. Cut yourself some slack, put the whip away, and love yourself as much as the people in your life love you.

Reaching Out

If you've been stigmatized, it's even harder to reach out. You may not believe that anyone will really be there for you. What if the person you reach out to is like others who have berated and abused you? There is always that chance. Yet that chance is minimized when you learn to pick people who will be there for you. Frequently the right people are those who are like you—people who have similar experiences to yours. They won't shame you because they know what it feels like. They may say something like, "I'm glad you called—listening to you reminds me of what I've been through," or "Thank you for reaching out to me," or "I know how you feel, it was so hard for me to reach out."

Reach out. Before you pick up the bottle, the loaf of bread, or your grandmother's pain pills, do something different. Reach outside your house of shame. Call a friend, family member, or therapist. Go to a 12-step meeting or support group. Don't let life kick your butt to the point that it's harder to get help. It's never too late. As long as you or your addictions don't kill you, there's hope. You have the courage inside of you to do it. Otherwise, you wouldn't have made it to this point in your life. You have the strength. You have the stamina to do the work to heal.

Now is the time to say yes. Say yes to a better future for yourself and those you love. The time is now. This is your time. Please take it.

APPENDIX A:

help
for
AD/HD
and
related
issues

AD/HD Websites

www.add.about.com
   Comprehensive information and resources

www.addandaddiction.com
   Wendy Richardson, MA, MFT, CAS

www.addcoaching.com
   ADDed Dimension Coaching Group

www.addconsults.com
   Resources and ADD consultations by Terry Matlen, MSW,
   ACSW

www.ADDvance.com
   Patricia Quinn, MD, and Kathleen Nadeau, PhD,
   information and support for women and girls

www.drhallowell.com
   Ned Hallowell, MD

www.nancyratey.com
   Nancy A. Ratey, EdM, ABDA, MCC, AD/HD coaching

www.sarisolden.com
   Sari Solden, MS, LMFT

Organizations

ADD Resources
    223 Tacoma Avenue S #100
    Tacoma, WA 98402
    253-759-5085
    Fax: 253-572-2470
    www.addresources.org
    E-mail: office@addresources.org

ADDA—National Attention Deficit Disorder Association
    P.O. Box 543
    Pottstown, PA 19464
    484-945-2101
    610-970-7520
    www.add.org
    E-mail: Mail@add.org

ADDISS—The National Attention Deficit Disorder Information
and Support Service (United Kingdom)
    P.O. Box 340
    Edgware
    Middlesex HA8 9HL
    020-8906-9068
    Fax: 020-8959-0727
    E-mail: info@addiss.co.uk

CHADD—Children and Adults with Attention Deficit Disorder
    8181 Professional Place, Suite 201
    Landover, MD 20785
    800-233-4050 or 301-306-7070
    Fax: 301-306-7090
    www.chadd.org

Kitty Petty ADD/LD Institute
    410 Sheridan Avenue, Suite 339
    Palo Alto, CA 94306-2020
    650-329-9443
    Fax: 650-321-5939
    www.kpinst.org
    E-mail: kitty@kpinst.org

Books

Amen, Daniel G., MD. *Change Your Brain, Change Your Life: The Breakthrough Program for Conquering Anxiety, Depression, Obsessiveness, Anger and Impulsiveness.* New York: Times Books, 1998.

Amen, Daniel G., MD. *Healing ADD: The Breakthrough Program That Allows You to See and Heal the 6 Types of ADD.* New York: Berkeley Publishing Group, 2001.

Brown, Thomas E., PhD. *Attention-Deficit Disorders and Comorbidities in Children, Adolescents, and Adults.* Washington, D.C.: American Psychiatric Press, Inc., 2000.

Fishbein, Diana H. *The Science, Treatment, and Prevention of Antisocial Behaviors, Application to the Criminal Justice System.* Kingston, N.J.: Civic Research Institute, 2000.

Chapter 16, "The Role of Genetics in ADHD and Conduct Disorder-Relevance to the Treatment of Recidivistic Antisocial Behavior," Comings, David E., MD.

Chapter 17, "Diagnosing and Treating ADHD in a Men's Prison," McCallon, Dwaine, MD.

Chapter 18, "Criminal Behavior Fueled by ADHD and Addiction," Richardson, Wendy, MA, MFT, CAS.

Hallowell, Edward M., MD, and John J. Ratey, MD. *Answers to Distraction.* New York: Pantheon Books, 2000.

Halverstadt, Jonathan, Scott, MS, MFT. *ADD & Romance: Finding Fulfillment in Love, Sex, & Relationships.* Dallas, Tex.: Taylor Trade Publishing, 1999.

Heller, Sharon, PhD. *Too Loud, Too Bright, Too Fast, Too Tight: What to Do If You Are Sensory Defensive in an Overstimulating World.* New York: Quill, 2003.

Kelly, Kate and Peggy Ramundo. *You Mean I'm Not Lazy, Stupid, or Crazy?* Cincinnati, Ohio: Tyrell and Jerem Press, 1993.

Kelly, Kate, Peggy Ramundo, and D. Steven Ledingham. *The ADDed Dimension—Daily Advice for ADD Adults.* New York: Simon & Schuster, 1997.

Kennedy, Diane M. *The ADHD Autism Connection: A Step Toward More Accurate Diagnosis and Effective Treatment.* Colorado Springs, Colo.: WaterBrook Press, 2002.

Latham, Peter S., and J. D. and Patricia H. Latham. *Attention Deficit Disorder and the Law: A Guide for Advocates.* JKL Communications, P.O. Box 40157, Washington D.C. 20016.

Ledingham, D. Steven. *The Scoutmaster's Guide to Attention Deficit Disorder: For Adults Working with Attention Deficit Disorder in Scouting and Other Youth Activities*, Second Edition. Tucson, Ariz.: Positive People Press, 1998.

Lehmkuhl, Dorothy and Dolores Cotter Lamping. *Organizing for the Creative Person.* New York: Crown Trade Paperbacks, 1993.

Nadeau, Kathleen G., PhD. *A Comprehensive Guide to Attention Deficit Disorder in Adults: Research, Diagnosis, Treatment.* New York: Brunner/Mazel, Inc., 1995.

Nadeau, Kathleen G., PhD, and Patricia O. Quinn, MD. *Understanding Women with AD/HD.* Silver Spring, Md.: Advantage Books, 2002.

Novotni, Michele, PhD, with Randy Petersen. *What Does Everybody Else Know That I Don't: Social Skills Help for Adults with Attention Deficit/Hyperactivity Disorder (AD/HD) A Reader-Friendly Guide.* Plantation, Fla.: Specialty Press, 1999.

Novotni, Michele, PhD, and Thomas A. Whiteman, PhD, with Randy Petersen. *Adult AD/HD: A Reader-Friendly*

Guide to Identifying, Understanding, and Treating Adult Attention Deficit/Hyperactivity Disorder. Colorado Springs, Colo.: Piñon Press, 2003.

Quinn, Patricia O., MD, and Kathleen G. Nadeau, PhD. *Gender Issues and AD/HD: Research, Diagnosis and Treatment.* Silver Spring, Md.: Advantage Books, 2002.

Quinn, Patricia O., Nancy A. Ratey, and Theresa L. Martland. *Coaching College Students with AD/HD: Issues and Answers.* Silver Springs, Md.: Advantage Books, 2000.

Ratey, John J., MD. *A User's Guide to the Brain: Perception, Attention, and the Four Theaters of the Brain.* New York: Pantheon Books, 2001.

Ratey, John J., MD, and Catherine Johnson, PhD. *Shadow Syndromes: Recognizing and Coping with the Hidden Psychological Disorders That Can Influence Your Behavior and Silently Determine the Course of Your Life.* New York: Pantheon Books, 1997.

Solden, Sari, M.S., M.F.C.C. *Journeys Through ADDulthood: Discover a New Sense of Identity and Meaning While Living with Attention Deficit Disorder.* New York: Walker and Company, 2002.

Soldon, Sari, MS, MFCC. *Women with Attention Deficit Disorder.* Grass Valley, Calif.: Underwood Books, 1995.

Weiss, Lynn Ph.D. *ADD on the Job: Making Your ADD Work for You.* Dallas, Tex.: Taylor Publishing, 1996.

Zeigler, Dendy, and Chris A. and Alex Zeigler. *A Bird's-Eye View of Life with ADD and ADHD: Advice from Young Survivors.* Cedar Bluff, Ala.: Cherish the Children, 2003.

AD/HD Periodicals
ADDitude
>   P.O. Box 421 2476
>   Bolsover Houston, TX 77005-2518
>   800-856-2032
>   www.additudemag.com

The ADHD Challenge
>   P.O. Box 2277
>   West Peabody, MA 01960-7277
>   800-233-2322
>   Fax: 978-535-3276
>   E-mail: adhdchlg@gis.net

Focus
>   ADDA—National Attention Deficit Disorder Association
>   P.O. Box 543
>   Pottstown, PA 19464
>   484-945-2101
>   Fax: 610-970-7520
>   www.add.org
>   E-mail: mail@add.org

APPENDIX B:

help
for
substance
abuse

Websites

Alcoholics Anonymous
www.aa.org—United States and Canada
www.alcoholics-anonymous.org.uk—England

Cocaine Anonymous
www.ca.org

Marijuana Anonymous
www.marijuana-anonymous.org

Narcotics Anonymous
www.na.org—United States and Canada
www.ukna.org—England

Books

Alcoholics Anonymous. *The Story of How Many Thousands of Men and Women Have Recovered from Alcoholism.* New York: Alcoholics Anonymous World Services, Inc., fourth edition, 2001.

Frey, James. *A Million Little Pieces*. New York: Random House, 2003.

Gorski, Terence T. and Merlene Miller. *Counseling for Relapse Prevention*. Independence, Mo.: Herald House-Independence Press, 1982.

McGovern, George. *Terry: My Daughter's Life and Death Struggle with Alcoholism*. New York: Penguin Books, 1996.

Narcotics Anonymous 3d ed., rev. Van Nuys, Calif.: World Service Office, Inc., 1986.

Newsletters and Publications

AA Grapevine: The International Monthly Journal of Alcoholics Anonymous
P.O. Box 1980
Grand Central Station, New York, NY 10163-1980.

The A.A. Member—Medications and Other Drugs.
New York: Alcoholics Anonymous World Services, Inc., 1984. Box 459, Grand Central Station, New York, NY 10163.

Addiction Professional
Manisses Communication Group, Inc.
208 Governor Street
Providence, RI 02906
800-333-7771
E-mail: manissescs@manisses.com

Counselor, The Magazine for Addiction Professionals.
Washington, D.C.: American Psychiatric Press.
800-368-5777
www.api.org
E-mail: order@appi.org

Questions & Answers on Sponsorship.
New York: Alcoholics Anonymous World Services, Inc., 1983. Box 459, Grand Central Station, New York, NY 10163.

Recovery Today, Institute of Chemical Dependency Studies
P.O. Box 565
Round Rock, TX 78680
512-246-6007
www.recoverytoday.net
E-mail: linda@cdstudies.com

Understanding Anonymity.
New York: Alcoholics Anonymous World Services, Inc.,
1981. Box 459,
Grand Central Station, New York, NY 10163.

Treatment Centers
Sierra Tucson—Arizona
Treatment for addictions, eating disorders, trauma,
anxiety disorders, and sexual compulsivity
800-842-4487
www.SierraTucson.com

Hazelden—Minnesota
800-257-7810
E-mail: info@hazelden.org

The Meadows—Arizona
Treatment for trauma, substance use disorders, anxiety
disorders, and sexual compulsivity
800-632-3697
www.themeadows.org

Betty Ford Center—California
Rancho Mirage, CA
760-773-4100
800-854-9211
www.bettyfordcenter.org

APPENDIX C:

Organizations and Websites

ANRED: Information and Resources
Information and resources for Anorexia nervosa, Bulimia, Binge eating, and other less-well-known eating disorders.
www.anred.com

Eating Disorders Association Home
Help, advice, and support to those suffering from Anorexia, Bulimia, Binge Eating, and other eating-related disorders.
www.edauk.com

New National Toll-Free Number for NEDIC
866-NEDIC-20 (866-63342-20)
or 416-340-4156 in Toronto

Books

Danowski, Debbie and Pedro Lazaro, MD. *Why Can't I Stop Eating?: Recognizing, Understanding and Overcoming Food Addiction*. Center City, Minn.: Hazelden, 2000.

Katherine, Anne. *Anatomy of a Food Addiction*. Carlsbad, Calif.: Gurze Books, 1991.

Normandi, Carol E. and Laurelee Roark. *It's Not About Food: Change Your Mind; Change Your Life; End Your Obsession with Food and Weight.* New York: The Berkeley Publishing Group, 1998.

Roth, Geneen. *Feeding the Hungry Heart.* New York: Penguin Group, 1982.

Roth, Geneen. *When Food Is Love: Exploring the Relationship Between Eating and Intimacy.* New York: Penguin Group, 1991.

Sheppard, Kay. *Food Addiction: The Body Knows,* rev. and expanded. Deerfield Beach, Fla.: Health Communications, 1993.

Somer, Elizabeth, MA, RD. *Food and Mood: The Complete Guide to Eating Well and Feeling Your Best.* New York: Henry Holt and Company, 1995.

APPENDIX D:

INTERNET ADDICTION
Websites
The Center for Internet Studies
   www.virtual-addiction.com

The Center for Online and Internet Addiction
   www.netaddiction.com

Books
Greenfield, David N., PhD. *Virtual Addiction: Help for Netheads, Cyberfreaks and Those Who Love Them.* Oakland, Calif.: New Harbinger Publications, 1999.

Young, Kimberly, PhD. *Caught in the Net: How to Recognize the Signs of Internet Addiction and a Winning Strategy for Recovery.* New Jersey: Wiley, 1998.

SEX AND LOVE ADDICTIONS
Websites
Dr. Patrick Carnes' Resources for Sex Addiction and Recovery
   www.sexhelp.com

Sex, Love, Relationship, and Pornography Addiction
http://open-mind.org/Sex-Love.htm

Books

Carnes, Patrick J., PhD. *Out of the Shadows: Understanding
Sexual Addiction.* Center City, Minn.: Hazeldon
Publishing, 2001.

Mellody, Pia, et. al. *Facing Love Addiction: Giving
Yourself the Power to Change the Way You Love.*
HarperSanFrancisco, 1989.

Young, Kimberly, PhD. *Tangled in the Web: Understanding
Cybersex from Fantasy to Addiction.* Bloomington, Ind.:
Authorhouse, 2001.

Treatment Centers

Sierra Tucson—Arizona
Treatment for addictions, eating disorders, trauma,
anxiety disorders, and sexual compulsivity
800-842-4487
http://www.SierraTucson.com

The Meadows—Arizona
Treatment for trauma, substance use disorders, anxiety
disorders, and sexual compulsivity
800-632-3697
www.themeadows.org

SHOPPING ADDICTION
Websites

4optimallife.com/Shopping-Addiction.html
An addiction exists. Just ask the person who has claimed
bankruptcy for the second time, the broken relationships
due to out of control spending/shopping.

http://www.addictions.co.uk/addiction.asp?id=shop
The consequences of shopping addiction are obvious: high
levels of debt, fear of discovery, and retribution leading to
more denial and desperate acts to cover it up.

www.indiana.edu/~engs/hints/shop.html
Control of compulsive shopping, spending addiction, or
shopaholism—a classical addictive behavior. Shopping
addiction tends to affect more women than men.

COMPULSIVE GAMBLING
Websites
Gamblers Anonymous
www.gamblersanonymous.org
International Service Office
P.O. Box 17173
Los Angeles, CA 90017
213-386-8789
Fax: 213-386-0030
E-mail: isomain@gamblersanonymous.org

National Council on Problem Gambling—Washington, D.C.
http:://www.ncpgambling.org.

Visit this website for referrals to residential treatment and
literature.
Email: ncpg@ncpgambling.org

New York Council On Problem Gambling
www.nyproblemgambling.org
119 Washington Avenue
Albany, NY 12210
The website is available in Spanish.
Helpline: 800-437-1611

From their website:

New York Council on Problem Gambling is a not-for-profit
independent corporation dedicated to increasing public
awareness about problem and compulsive gambling
and advocating for support services and treatment for
persons adversely affected by gambling. The Helpline
(in NYS 1-800-437-1611) provides 24-hour staffed daily
telephone coverage, supportive intervention, and resource
and referral information to persons seeking assistance
regarding problem gambling.

EXERCISE ADDICTIONS
Websites
http://www.eatingproblems.org/epsexer.html

Exercise addiction is common in anorectics and bulimics, because they think that excessive exercise can help them get thin.

http://www.internet-articles.com/nutrition

Fitness & Nutrition Articles Hooked on the Pain: Exercise Addiction. Exercise addiction is an eating disorder like anorexia and bulimia.

NOTES

CHAPTER 2

1. Daniel G. Amen, MD, *Healing ADD: The Breakthrough Program That Allows You to See and Heal the 6 Types of ADD* (New York: Berkeley, 2001), p. XV.
2. Thomas E. Brown, PhD, *Attention-Deficit Disorders and Comorbidities in Children, Adolescents, and Adults* (Washington, D.C.: American Psychiatric Press, 2000), p. 321.

CHAPTER 4

1. John Ratey, MD, and Catherine Johnson, PhD, *Shadow Syndromes: Recognizing and Coping with the Hidden Psychological Disorders That Can Influence Your Behavior and Silently Determine the Course of Your Life* (New York City: Pantheon, 1997), p. 279.
2. Ronald Kotulak, *Inside the Brain: Revolutionary Discoveries of How the Mind Works* (Kansas City, Mo.: Andrews and McMeel, 1996), p. 107.

CHAPTER 6

1. W. W. Dodson, *The Prevalence and Treatment of Sleep Disorders in Adults with Attention Deficit/Hyperactivity Disorder* (Washington, D.C.: Presented at the 152nd Annual Meeting of the American Psychiatric Association, 1999).

2. Kathleen G. Nadeau, PhD, and Patricia O. Quinn, MD, *Gender Issues and AD/HD Research, Diagnosis and Treatment* (Silver Spring, Md.: Advantage Books, 2002), p. 358.

   Q. R. Regestein and M. Pavlova, "Treatment of Delayed Sleep Phase Syndrome," *General Hospital Psychiatry* 17 (1995): 335-345.
3. Sharon Heller, PhD, *Too Loud, Too Bright, Too Fast, Too Tight: What to Do If You Are Sensory Defensive in an Overstimulating World* (New York: HarperCollins, 2003), p. 3.

CHAPTER 7
1. Edward M. Hallowell, MD, and John J. Ratey, MD, *Driven to Distraction* (New York: Pantheon, 1994), p. 195.
2. J. Biederman, E. Mick, J. Q. Bostic, J. Prince, J. Daly, T. E. Wilens, T. Spenser, J. Garcia-Jetton, R. Russell, J. Wozniak, and S. V. Faraone, "The Naturalistic Course of Pharmacologic Treatment of Children with Manic Like Symptoms: A Systematic Chart Review," *Journal of Clinical Psychiatry* 59 (1998): 628-637.

   K. D. Chang, H. Steiner, and T. A. Ketter, "Psychiatric Phenomenology of Child and Adolescent Bipolar Offspring," *Journal of the American Academy of Child and Adolescent Psychiatry* 39 (2000): 453-360.
3. Kathleen G. Nadeau, PhD, and Patricia O. Quinn, MD, *Gender Issues and AD/HD Research, Diagnosis and Treatment* (Silver Spring, Md.: Advantage Books, 2002), p. 366.
4. Conversation with T. Dwain McCallon, MD, 2004. Printed with permission.

CHAPTER 8
1. Daniel G. Amen, MD, *A Clinician's Guide to Understanding and Treating Attention Deficit Disorder (Childhood Through Adulthood)* (Fairfield, Calif.: MindWorks Press, 1995).
2. K. Blum, J. Cull, E. Braverman, and D. Comings, "Reward Deficiency Syndrome," *American Scientist* 84 (1996): 132-145.

Bonci, G. Bernardi, P. Grillner, and N. B. Mercuri, "The Dopamine-containing Neuron: Maestro or Simple Musician in the Orchestra of Addiction," *Trends Pharmacological Science* 24, 4, 172 (April 2003).

Eric J. Nestler and Robert C. Malenka, "The Addicted Brain," *Scientific American* (March 2004): 78-85.

3. One study by the NIAAA analyzed the genotype of 204 male and female college students who fit the criterion for binge drinking, five or more drinks for men, and four or more for women. Researchers focused on the serotonin transporter gene (5-HTT). They found a long and a short version of this gene. We inherit one gene from each of our parents, which means we can inherit two long genes, two short genes, or one long and one short. Interestingly, those who carried two of the short version of the serotonin transporting gene binged on alcohol, drank to get drunk, and drank more alcohol at occasions than the students with the other genotypes. The article "Serotonin transporter promoter polymorphism and differences in alcohol consumption behavior in a college student population" is published as a Rapid Communication at http://alcalc.oupjournals.org.

4. Ronald Kotulak, *Inside the Brain: Revolutionary Discoveries of How the Mind Works* (Kansas City, Mo.: Andrews and McMeel, 1996), p. 71.

5. J. M. Oldham, E. Hollander, and A. E. Skodal, *Impulsivity and Compulsivity* (Arlington, Va.: American Psychiatric Press, Inc., 1990).

6. Blum, Cull, Braverman, and Comings, "Reward Deficiency Syndrome," *American Scientist* 84 (1996): 132-145.

7. Eric J. Nestler and Robert C. Malenka, "The Addicted Brain," *Scientific American* (March 2004): 85.

8. Blum, Cull, Braverman, and Comings, "Reward Deficiency Syndrome," *American Scientist* 84 (1996): 132-145.

9. A. Bonci, G. Bernardi, P. Grillner, and N. B. Mercuri, "The Dopamine-containing Neuron: Maestro or Simple Musician in the Orchestra of Addiction," *Trends Pharmacological Science* 24, 4, 172 (April 2003).

10. Eric J. Nestler and Robert C. Malenka, "The Addicted Brain," *Scientific American* (March 2004): 82-85.

11. Thompson, Riggs, Mikulich, and Crowley, "Contribution of ADHD symptoms to substance abuse problems and

delinquency in conduct-disordered adolescent," *Journal of Abnormal Child Psychology* 24 (1996): 325-347.

12. J. Biederman, T. Wilens, E. Mick, S. V. Faraone, W. Weber, S. Curtis, A. Thornell, Pfister, K. Jetton, and J. G. and J. Soriano, "Is ADHD a Risk Factor for Psychoactive Substance Use Disorders? Findings from a Four-Year Prospective Follow-up Study," *Journal of the American Academy of Child and Adolescent Psychiatry* 36 (1997): 21-29.

CHAPTER 9

1. J. Biederman, T. Wilens, E. Mick, S. V. Faraone, W. Weber, S. Curtis, A. Thornell, Pfister, K. Jetton, and J. G. and J. Soriano, "Is ADHD a Risk Factor for Psychoactive Substance Use Disorders? Findings from a Four-Year Prospective Follow-up Study," *Journal of the American Academy of Child and Adolescent Psychiatry* 36 (1997): 21-29.

   J. Biederman, T. Wilens, E. Mick, et. al., "Does Attention-Deficit Hyperactivity Disorder Impact the Development Course of Drug and Alcohol Abuse and Dependence," *Biol Psychiatry* 44 (1997): 269-273.

2. Di Marzo, T. Bisogno, and L. De Petrocellis, "Endocannabinoids: New Targets for Drug Development," Instituto per la Chimica di Molecole di Interesse Biologico, Consiglio Nazionale delle Ricerche, Via Toiano 6, 80072, Arco Felice, Napoli, Italy. *Curr Pharm Des* Sep; 6 (2000): 1361-1381.

CHAPTER 10

1. Kathleen G. Nadeau, PhD, and Patricia O. Quinn, MD, *Gender Issues and AD/HD Research, Diagnosis and Treatment* (Silver Spring, Md.: Advantage Books, 2002), pp. 412-426.

   Fleming, John, PhD, Levy, Lance. M.B., Chapter 20, Eating Disorders in Women with AD/HD, pp. 412-426.

2. L. D. Levy, *Conquering Obesity: Deceptions in the Marketplace and the Real Story* (Toronto, Can.: Key Porter Books, 2000).

3. Elizabeth Somer, MA, RD, *Food and Mood: The Complete Guide to Eating Well and Feeling Your Best* (New York: Henry Holt and Company, 1995), p. 248.

4. G. J. Wang, N. D. Volkow, J. Logan, N. R. Pappas, C. T. Wong, W. Shu, N. Netsulil, and J. Fowler, "Brain Dopamine

and Obesity," *The Lancet* (February 3, 2001) 9271: 1883, pp. 354-357.

5. Colantuoni C, Schwenker J, McCarthy J, Rada P, Ladenheim B, Cadet JL, Schwartz GJ, Moran TH, Hoebel BG., (2001) Excessive sugar intake alters binding to dopamine and mu-opioid receptors in the brain. *Neuroreport*, (Princeton University Press, Princeton, New Jersey, Nov. 16; 12 (16): 3529-52.)

6. C. Colantuoni, P. Rada, J. McCarthy, C. Patten, N. M. Avena, A. Chadeayne, and B. G. Hoebel, "Evidence That Intermittent, Excessive Sugar Intake Causes Endogenous Opioid Dependence" (Princeton, N.J.: Princeton University Press, 2002), *Obes. Res.* June; 10(6): 478-488.

CHAPTER 11

1. Kenneth Blum, Peter J. Sheridan, Robert C. Wood, Eric R. Braverman, Chen, and J. H. Thomas, "Dopamine D2 Receptor Gene Variants: Association and Linkage Studies in Impulsive-Addictive-Compulsive Behavior," *Pharmacogenetics*, vol. 5 (1995).

CHAPTER 13

1. Conversation with D. Steven Ledingham, 2004. Printed by permission.

2. Kathleen G. Nadeau, PhD, and Patricia O. Quinn, MD, *Gender Issues and AD/HD Research, Diagnosis and Treatment* (Silver Spring, Md.: Advantage Books, 2002), p. 355.

W. W. Dodson, "The Prevalence and Treatment of Sleep Disorders in Adults with Attention Deficit/Hyperactivity Disorder" (Presented at the 152nd Annual Meeting of the American Psychiatric Association, Washington, D.C., 1999).

CHAPTER 14

1. J. Biederman, T. Wilens, E. Mick, S. V. Faraone, W. Weber, S. Curtis, A. Thornell, K. Pfister, J. G. Jetton, and J. Soriano, "Is ADHD a Risk Factor for Psychoactive Substance Use Disorders? Findings from a Four-Year Prospective Follow-up Study," *Journal of the American Academy of Child and Adolescent Psychiatry* 36 (1997): 21-29.

L. Hechtman, "Adolescent Outcome of Hyperactive Children Treated with Stimulants in Childhood: A Review," *Psychopharmacol Bull* 21 (1985): 178-191.

2. L. Hechtman and G. Weiss, "Controlled Prospective Fifteen Year Follow-up of Hyperactives as Adults: Non Medical Drug and Alcohol Use and Anti-social Behavior," *Can J. Psychiatry* 31 (1986): 557.

3. Timothy E. Wilens, MD, et. al., "Does Stimulant Therapy of Attention-Deficit/Hyperactivity Disorder Beget Later Substance Abuse? A Meta-analytic Review of the Literature," *Journal of Pediatrics* (January 2003; 111(1)): 179-185.

4. Wilens, pp. 179-185.

5. Edward M. Hallowell, MD, and John J. Ratey, MD, *Driven to Distraction* (New York: Pantheon, 1994), p. 237.

6. J. Biederman, T. E. Wilens, E. Mick, et. al., "Protective Effects of ADHD Pharmacotherapy on Substance Abuse: A Longitudinal Study," *Pediatrics* (1999) 104(2): 20.

7. Hallowell and Ratey, p. 237.

8. Alcoholics Anonymous World Service, Inc., *The AA Member—Medications and Other Drugs* (New York: 1984).

9. Terence T. Gorski and Merlene Miller, *Counseling for Relapse Prevention* (Independence, Mo.: Herald House-Independence, 1982).

CHAPTER 15

1. Terence T. Gorski and Merlene Miller, *Counseling for Relapse Prevention* (Independence, Mo.: Herald House-Independence, 1982).

2. P. H. Wender, D. R. Wood, and F. W. Reinherr, "Pharmacological Treatment of Attention-Deficit Disorder, Residual Type (ADD, RT, Minimal Brain Dysfunction, Hyperactivity in Adults)," *Psychopharmacol Bull* 21: (1985) 222-227.

S. L. Satel and J. C. Nelson, "Stimulants in the Treatment of Depression: A Critical Review," *Journal of Clinical Psychiatry* 50 (1989): 241-249.

INDEX

ABOUT
THE AUTHOR

WENDY RICHARDSON, MA, MFT, CAS, is a Licensed Marriage and Family Therapist and Certified Addiction Specialist in private practice in Soquel, California. Wendy is the author of *The Link Between ADD & Addiction, Getting the Help You Deserve*, Piñon Press (1997). She has contributed chapters on AD/HD and co-occurring addictions to books focusing on criminology, and women with AD/HD.

Wendy has devoted the last decade of her thirty-year career in mental health to treating people with AD/HD and co-occurring addictions, eating disorders, and behavioral addictions. She is inspired and motivated by her personal and professional passion to help others whose lives have also been affected by AD/HD and addiction. Wendy believes that educating others about AD/HD through her writing, international speaking, and trainings is a huge step toward smashing stigmas, reducing shame, and helping people get the treatment they deserve.

Wendy lives in a beach town in northern California. She is an avid rock and mountain climber. Her other passion is photography. Wendy and her children travel whenever and wherever possible. They enjoy meeting new people, skiing, snowboarding, hiking, and finding new trails wherever they go.

THERE IS HOPE.